PRAISE FOR *CREAT*

A book that speaks to the heart of creative life that matters. Inspiring and pragmatic, Jess clears away the weeds to reveal a clear path to engage the real art and convergence of play and point of view.

--Michael Fields
Producing Artistic Director, Dell'Arte

"It's possible that Jess believes in you more than you do. Like a hug from a smart, caring, mentor, this book will go a long way to getting you moving."

-- Seth Godin
Author, The Icarus Deception

Jess Pillmore wants to revolutionize the way we experience learning about the arts. Using the notion of creating ensemble-- which applies to anyone who works in relationship to another--she wants to help you create a place and method where fear is banished and your instincts and intelligence are in harmony with others and your own self interests. Inspirational, informative and personal, this book will help any arts educator, artist or collaborator understand what makes for healthy learning environments.

-- Kira Obolensky
Writer and Educator

Deeply uplifting as a good friendship is, this book embraces you with the good energy and creative solutions of Jess Pillmore. As you get to know her ideas for nurturing creativity, you get to know her too, and you realize you have found a companion with a shared goal, that of nurturing the life spirit common to all constructive human endeavors. I will recommend this book to many people.

-- Judith Fox-Fliesser, M.D.
Psychiatrist, Psychoanalyst, Artist

Who am I and how do I want to live my life?' In this artist's manifesto Jess Pillmore puts this challenge to all who want to live a Creatively Independent life. Independent of judgement, creative in the broadest sense, encircled by the positive reinforcement of an "ensemble" of others. This is not just a workbook for theatre types, but for everyone ready to embrace creative, community-focused and playful life choices based in hope not fear.

-- Gail M. Burns
Theatre Critic

What if our decision making was driven by our understanding of consequence rather than Right/Wrong or Good/Bad? I believe there is an inherent responsibility in Consequence that Right/Wrong or Good/Bad don't carry because of their subjective nature. What Jess Pillmore is outrageously, poetically and inspiringly suggesting is that if we are willing to be responsible for the Consequence of our actions, we are free to make the choices we have yet to dream of making and in so doing open the floodgates of creativity and cooperation within ourselves and those around us. This just might lead to a world where the 'golden rule' is not a quote but a way.

-- Daniel Stein
Clinical Professor, Head of Movement and Physical Theatre
Brown Univ./Trinity Rep. MFA Acting Program

Jess' book is an incredibly practical and inspiring workbook on how to jumpstart your creativity. She speaks to the heart and challenges of making art and putting yourself out there. I felt reminded and challenged to face my habits and fears head-on and forge my own creative independence.

-- Christine Brubaker
Award-winning Stage and Screen Actor,
Arts Educator, Director

CREATIVELY INDEPENDENT

Life On Your Terms With Play, Community, and Awareness

CREATIVELY
INDEPENDENT

Life on Your Terms
With Play, Community, and Awareness

1st Edition

Jess Pillmore

Creatively Independent, llc
Revolutionary. Arts. Education.
CreativelyIndependent.net

Creatively Independent: Life on Your Terms with Play, Community and Awareness - Edition #1 (2012)

Published by Creatively Independent, llc

Designed by Jess Pillmore.

We all process information differently so I've made the manifesto available as an ebook and audiobook. Find them online at CreativelyIndependent.net

Join our digital ensemble @ CreativelyIndependent.net/blog

ISBN-13: 978-1-48203-392-2

"If you have come here to help me,
you are wasting your time.
But if you have come because your
liberation is bound up with mine
then let us work together."

Aboriginal activists group, Queensland, 1970s

THANK YOU

To all those with the courage to actively claim your own point of view. Thank you for embracing the opportunity to risk, fail, play and succeed together on our individual journeys. Thank you to my family and friends for their support, perspective and love. This manifesto would not have been possible with you all.

A SPECIAL THANK YOU TO:

Devora Neumark, for her passion, vulnerability and original response to this project, "You can write your manifesto in a few weeks, then what are you going to do with it?"

Kira Obolensky, for her gentle nudging as I walked closer to the edge of what I *know*.

Seth Godin, for his generosity, poignant advice, hard deadlines and constant inspiration.

Chris Beaulieu, for his passion and "If not now, then when?" mantra.

Griffin, for the motivation and the playfulness.

Ron Morris, for asking me "What's the heart of your art?"

Dewin Barnette, for her eye for story in text and image.

Sara Nolan, editor rockstar, for her humor and high bar.

My parents, Jo & Bill, for their unwavering support and unconditional love.

My early readers, for all their wonderful insight. You helped me with every revision.

TABLE OF CONTENTS

INTRODUCTION

SELF-AWARENESS

THE ENSEMBLE

RHYTHMIC REVOLUTION

CREATIVE CYCLES

INTRODUCTION

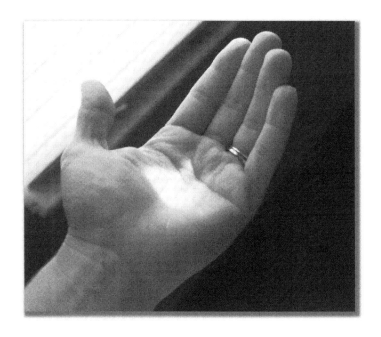

My Intention

YOUR IRREFUTABLE RIGHT

We ALL have the irrefutable right to be independent, meaning that we are not relying on or subject to any of the following life-limiting fears:

* Fear of Not Being Picked
* Fear of Perfection
* Fear of Imperfection
* Fear of Shaking the Boat
* Fear of Judgment
* Fear of Failure
* Fear of Humiliation
* Fear of Wasted Time
* Fear of Rejection
* Fear of the Spotlight
* Fear of Never Being Noticed
* Fear of Not Being Up to the Challenge
* Fear of Taking a Risk
* Fear of Loving Someone Else or Yourself

We ALL have the inherent ability to sculpt the world around us with our creativity. This powerful part of our being is untapped potential waiting to be strengthened, expanded and inspired by ourselves, our dreams and those around us.

MY INTENTION
Why? Why this? Why this now?

Intention is key. *Why* someone does something is as important, if not more important, than what one does. My artistic work relies heavily on understanding and owning one's intention. So it is true to the spirit of reciprocity and mutuality in this manifesto to start this book with my clearest intention for myself and for you.

I WANT TO:
Strive towards living in a centered world.

Switch from knee-jerk reactions to conscious choices.

Balance information with internal understanding.

Feel at the helm of my life, not at the beck and call of others.

Accept others for who they are right now on their journeys.

Love myself, where I am right now on my journey.

The more I put it off, the more these wants become needs. I need this change in myself in order to be healthier, happier, more creative and centered in this rapidly-evolving world.

If you feel the need for a more centered life...
I wrote this for you too.

If you feel pulled in multiple directions...
I wrote this for you too.

If you are becoming cynical, but don't want to...
I wrote this for you too.

If you know in your heart you should be making your
own choices...
I wrote this for you too.

If you love your dreams and want to make them
realities...
I wrote this for you too.

If you want to discover and own your process in life...
I wrote this for you too.

I'm curious about what could be possible in a world
where people take responsibility for their choices, are
actively releasing themselves from life-limiting fears,
and are conscious of how they work together.

If you feel the need for such a world...
I wrote this for you too.

EXPERIENTIAL LEARNING
How to use this manifesto

This manifesto was written to encourage, provoke, and offer a way of envisioning what life can be when we are no longer requiring, relying on, or subject to our life-limiting fears. It is a call to action to creatively sculpt the world around us through play, community, and awareness. It is a call to stop giving weight to fears that keep us from taking life-enriching risks and start embracing that which makes each of us unique and invaluable.

The time is now because in the world around us, where fear is so tangible, calming our fears has joined the ranks of basic needs like eating, sleeping, and finding shelter. To add to the confusion, scientists are showing that we are hardwired to meet short-term needs before long-term (and often more wholesome) needs.

So, if fears are being confused with needs, then short-term fears become the loudest. No wonder that unexpected phone call from your ex keeps you up at night instead of, say, pondering whether you'll have healthy teeth when you're ninety.

In order to change our long-term journey for the better, we need to rewire how we respond to the short-term fears. Studies show, time and again, that we are in fact addicted to *fear itself*. But there's no need to wean ourselves from our fears *by ourselves*.

Humans are interdependent creatures. We need accountability. We need a group to bounce our questions and self-observations off of. This group will ask us a deeper, non-judgmental "Why?":

Why are you doing this?
Why did you focus on that?
Why did you hold that belief?
Why did you think that was suppose to be the outcome?
Why did you pick me to partner with?

Churn out those *Why's* like a bouncy 3-year old does! (It's the simplest question that can open up a world of understanding.) We need to be able to offer that same sounding board to others. This work does not happen in a bubble.

This is why there are support groups for virtually any endeavor or recovery effort. For our process, we will call this your "ensemble".

Your ensemble helps you with the little steps that make the long journey possible.

Set up your ensemble now. List a few people—or even just one—who can be there for you unconditionally on this journey. Can you reciprocate this presence?

Do you need to find people to work with on this journey? Visit the online forum to connect, interact and move forward in the work.

Each section addresses and explores elements of your creatively independent process, your point of view, and your ability to creatively explore the world around you with others. The manifesto is divided into the following parts:

* **Self-Awareness** - Who are you right now?
* **The Ensemble** - How does your group help you? How do you help your group?
* **Rhythmic Revolution** - What tools, or rhythms, can you explore to become more creatively independent?
* **Creative Cycles** - How do you support the on-going creative process within you and your ensemble?

This manifesto was written to be part of your ensemble: to sit with you, poke at you, laugh with you, and challenge you. After each section there are "Self-Observation" questions for you to consider solo and with your ensemble. They are meant to be writing prompts, conversation starters, and even themes for creative projects. They are offerings through which you can make the manifesto your own, relevant to your present outlook on life. So take your time with this book: read, play, and process.

Feel where the manifesto rubs you wrong. Observe where you nod your head in agreement. Breathe. Observe your breath. Take your time.

USING SELF-OBSERVATION
No, It's Not Navel Gazing

Self-observation is a tool for assessing how you *really* feel about a given situation. Your body and your emotions are tried-and-true messengers. They are your internal ensemble, continuously supplying you with valuable feedback. If you wish to hear the answers, you have to observe and listen to what they tell you, see it for what it is, and feel what you're *actually* feeling (and not, perhaps, what you wish you were feeling).

INTRODUCTION

Most of the time we rush through life. Time is a form of currency and we can feel as if we live in a debt-burdened (inner) world. Or we assume despondently that a debt-ridden world has been shaped for us, and we must try to figure out how to afford to live in it.

We can change that by taking the time to self-observe. Aren't your health, happiness, and independence worth not having to declare time-bankruptcy?

Self-observation is scientific and nonjudgmental. See if you can break down each moment of embodied reaction by assessing your physical responses to stimuli: breath, heart rate, body tension, gaze, posture, body language, internal dialog, etc. Assess the quality of *you* in the quality of the moment.

Often we jump right to judgment (good vs. bad) or conjecture (unfounded conclusions). Judgment lives in the past. It holds up your current position against past experiences or information and then assigns (warped) value accordingly. Conjecture lives in the future. It holds your current position against what might come of it, the "what if's" that lie ahead. It then assigns value to your current action, weighing the risk against the imagined (or feared) outcome.

The impulses of judgment and conjecture are both an angel and devil perched on each shoulder, overly quick to evaluate your current situation. Self-observation means locating the real you, smack in the middle of the present moment—what you are seeing, feeling, and taking in.

It could look something like this (and beware of writing off the mundane as *insignificant* too quickly):

Right now, writing these words, I observe myself scratching my head and shaking my foot. I observe a dull pain in the left side of my back. I observe the aroma of food and my growling stomach. I observe my head nodding in time with a song in my earphones. I observe my typing is sporadic.

From self-observation comes the next step: asking *why?*

Why do I find myself *just like this* in the present moment?

Your response will inevitably blend considerations of past and future (judgment and conjecture) with real data. For example, from my self-observation I decide I've been sitting long enough in this chair typing, leaning on my left side—either because I'm right-handed or because the window's on my left and I'm "leaning toward" being outside. I'm hungry. This song makes me want to dance. And I've slowed down my typing because I might be feeling self-conscious (and so hesitant) about making my own self-observations transparent in this chapter.

So, what's the big take-away? I learned what I need to move forward consciously into the next moment. I'm going to stretch and get a bite to eat.

SELF-OBSERVATION:
Manifesto, I Observe that I'm Observing Right Now

Do you self-observe regularly? Occasionally? Rarely?

How do you assess your actions? By your emotions? Physical states? The reactions?

When you make self-observations, does it slip into judgment?

When someone asks you "How are you?" do you answer truthfully or politely?

What does it take to stop and self-observe on any given day?

As an exercise, observe yourself right now: physically--heart rate, quality of breath, intensity of gaze, body tension/ease, emotions, mental-chatter (your inner-dialogue).

It's important to practice self-observation in neutral scenarios. With repetition, the roll-call of internal ensemble members will become second nature. This way you can access self-observation in more stressful or fearful scenarios, when you "really need" the answers.

How does it feel to address these questions?

WORTH IT

Before you can call on your ensemble, you have to do the first step on your own. The step of saying, "This is enough—enough boredom, frustration, pain, sadness and feeling less-than. Enough." The remaining steps will be in the company of your ensemble of like-hearted individuals, who are living different examples of the same goal: being creatively independent.

Living life creatively independent of life-limiting fear and surrounded by a supportive community is worth it.

You are worth it.

I encourage you to:

* Get your ensemble together.

* Set up regular meetings.

* Set goals, deadlines, projects. This work reveals itself in the play, in the creation, in the *doing*. There are tasks suggested to encourage play. The body cannot lie, so get it involved in this process and listen to what it has to say.

* Step fully into the work. Don't tiptoe; even if you only complete one exercise or section each day/week/ month, commit to that moment with your full attention and playfulness.

* Write in the margins of this book. It is yours to use as you need.

* Start a notebook. Whether this means journaling, doodling, or gathering photos, the physical act of expressing yourself helps you own your experiences. It also helps you own and articulate your future.

* Breathe. Observe your breath. The simple act of inhaling and exhaling, holding your breath, yawning, etc. can inform you on how you are taking in the moment and what you are open to.

* Add your own Self-Observation Questions, if questions come to you that are not on the list.

* Send them in to be considered for the next edition of the manifesto.

* If you want to interact with a global ensemble, post your questions online in our forum.

* Document your discoveries. The documentation could be as simple as a sentence on a scrap of paper, or as in-depth as a blog. This allows you to step back and see your discoveries. Sharing what you find also

allows you and your ensemble to move forward *together*.

* Take your time, but be diligent. Lean into the work. It will be a different process for everyone. Only you know when to move into the next section, or when to revisit a previous one.

> "When our gift is unwrapped,
> the whole community benefits."
> — Thea Elijah

THE MANY POWERS OF YOUR ENSEMBLE

Amazing feats can be accomplished with the healthy support of your ensemble and a creative outlook, which we *all* can access. This chapter describes some of the benefits of having an ensemble and how to intentionally gather them together.

Your ensemble understands and challenges you. They are healthy influences. They inspire and surprise you. They respond and encourage your true nature and intention. They get you *and* they get at you. Although each member may focus on different points on the horizon, a sustainable ensemble embraces their different modes of learning, exploring, and playing to empathize and encourage.

Your ensemble members will most likely not all be of your generation, your sex, your culture, your race, your location, your economic bracket or your occupation. If you look for them solely in familiar places or categories, then you'll find only more of the known. In order to support, challenge, and expand yourself, you need to go into the unknown too.

The members of a beneficial ensemble are found sprinkled throughout time and place: where you are, where you were and, most importantly, where you want to be.

I mean this literally and figuratively. Your ensemble can be gathered based on location, project, interest, etc. For example, because of how I like to work, play and be inspired, my main ensemble is constructed like this:

"Where I was" THEN
- Friends and Family - A select group of people who have a history with me but can still see me in

the present moment. It's a delicate balance and there are a select few in this group.

- Past Mentors - Another small group of educators in various fields that share a common passion for play, ownership, and high stakes. We know one another's process and influences and yet can stay current and forward-leaning in the work. Some have died, and yet I still look back on their advice for guidance in my ensemble.

"Where I am" NOW

- Community Artists (musicians, visual artists, writers, actors, circus performers, dancers, directors, and choreographers) in the pockets of the world where I create art.
- Like-Minded Seekers - people of any age searching for more answers inside progressive education. These people don't necessarily live near me, but we connect online through forums.
- Collaborators - Artists, educators, friends, and strangers whom I currently create with in my different fields of theatre, dance, education, creative writing, business, and music.

"Where I want to be" SOON

- Innovators - Because I want to live on the leading edge of my work, this section of my ensemble is vital. Some are innovators in their career, some in their everyday lives. Some are people I've had the honor of engaging with, like Seth Godin, Kathleen Marshall, and Gregory Hines. Some are influences from afar, like Brené Brown, Aaron Sorkin, Simon McBurney, Julie Taymor, Sir Ken Robinson, and Malcolm Gladwell.

Many of the members of my ensemble don't fit into one category. They float between categories, depending on how our relationship changes, or they straddle many categories because of the nature of my work with them. For example, my three-year old son Griffin is in both my Now and Soon category. He challenges and inspires me in the moment, but he also gives me opportunities and reasons for leaning forward into my future. My little muse will be popping up in this manifesto a bunch.

We can be a part of many different ensembles at once depending on our needs and our contributions to the group. Our level of engagement can also vary depending on the ensemble. How many you are a part of, or how you interact with your ensemble(s) is a personal choice with unique outcomes. The important part is that you recognize your groups and make conscious connections.

Ensemble Roll Call

Who's in your ensemble now? Remember to consider those that you may have not personally met but who's work or life choices inspire you.

Take a moment to list out your current support network. Then ask yourself how they contribute to your ensemble:

Who would you add to your ensemble?

See what might be needed or missing from the above ensemble. List more people to engage with in your ensemble. Here are a few prompts to get you going:

Who inspires you?

Who challenges you?

Who has your back?

Who calls your bluff?

Who do you enjoy helping?

Who do you aspire to work with or meet in the future?

How does it feel to ask yourself these questions?

SELF-
AWARENESS

I Am

I AM... WHO DO YOU NEED ME TO BE?

Ever played the party game *Guess Who?* The host puts a sticker on your back with the name of a celebrity or fictional character. You have to figure out who you are by how the other guests interact with you, or through answering Yes or No questions.

That was me, trying to figure out... me. Except, instead of a sticker on my back, there was a little mirror. So, people would meet me. Look at my back to see who I "was." But instead of seeing "Jess Pillmore", they would see themselves in the tiny mirror. They would answer my searching questions from their own perspectives. Meanwhile, I was trying to integrate every clue they gave, thinking they would show me who *I* was, when in fact they were giving me clues to who *they* were. Not much of a party in the long run.

I was highly adept at being what I thought people needed me to be at any given moment. I became a social chameleon for the same reason a little reptile does: a defense based on fear. I was relying on my amygdala, the brain's control center for fear responses, for more life choices than it was ever designed for.

The amygdala, located in the limbic system, is linked to some powerful motivators: emotions and fear responses. It is also in charge of arousal, secreting hormones, and forming emotional memories. It is there to help us survive and thrive.

Fear is your secret service agency. Fear is not your CEO.

Since the amygdala wields powerful and overwhelming tools (hormones are complicated creatures), it can be hard to distinguish between different forms of arousal: "Ahhh! There's a lion in the bushes!" or "Ahhh! My boss just called an unscheduled meeting!" or "Ahhh! I forgot to do the laundry!"

It's up to us to observe and assess in order to teach our amygdala the difference.

By 22 years-old, I was already skipping ahead of my game plan faster than many thought possible. I was carried on a tidal wave of success and opportunity, smack in the middle of New York City: choreographing Off-Broadway, working behind the scenes of major Broadway theaters and television companies, and rising to the top-three for interviews to assist Broadway choreographers. I was tap-dancing on quicksand, never giving myself a moment to ask honestly "Why does this feel wrong?" and then listen courageously for the answer.

But it did "feel wrong." In response, I began retreating inwardly, canceling dates, pushing responsibilities to the side, and avoiding making decisions in general.

Then I stopped. Literally.

I shut-down, stopped everything I knew and sat silently for, well, over a year. I went into survival mode.

The world was spinning frantically, or was that me doing the spinning? Every choice felt so dire that I made absolutely no choices whatsoever—except to start straight ahead. And I am ever-thankful for that. The dancer's instinct to focus on one spot on the horizon for balance and clarity kicked in and kept me from losing all my bearings.

That point in the distance was the phrase "Creatively Independent." This label wasn't equivalent to "Broadway director/choreographer"; it was more complex than that. It was how I wanted to be able to introduce myself, but I didn't have the courage. So I did the next closest thing: when my husband, Chris

Beaulieu, and I established our arts education company, we gave it the mission and name *Creatively Independent.*

Deep down, I wanted to believe myself to be creatively independent. But to do that meant I had to investigate dependence, independence, and interdependence. I spent too long depending on life-limiting fears to call the shots in my life and my art. Fictional fears of others' expectations, fears of running out of time, fears of "being discovered as a phony", fears of never being discovered at all... the list was long. The detours and time-outs I took in life were mostly unconscious or reactionary.

I wasn't tapping into the true support of the vibrant, interdependent world around me. I felt the need for ensemble, but I had been "trained" out of that need: everywhere I had worked and learned, there was a clear status division between teacher and student. The message was consistently "Follow *these pre-fab* steps to achieve your dreams", work hard, and, in your spare time, work even harder. This message was reinforced through assessment tests, auditions, and the tone of interviews in my professional life. At each of these moments, *someone else* held the key to the next level on my path—to reach this key, I was training to jump higher, sing louder and smile brighter than everyone else.

But it was exhausting and lonely. I was literally breaking down from the strain of my training and the expectations attached to it. I couldn't let others dictate my path anymore.

I was an over-achiever, in my early twenties, and in the middle of amazing opportunities and success, but I realized the real question wasn't "How can I achieve my goals?" It was "Why are these my goals, my community, my life choices?" And even deeper, "Have I chosen them or have they been chosen for me?" I had to own my path, a path of artistic creation and ultimate focus that had not been mapped out and navigated by anyone else.

For me, there were many pieces that had to fall into place to help me discovery the key concepts in this book: play, awareness, community, etc. Some of those pieces were painful. Some were the best experiences of my life to date. Some were random to the point of being explainable only by cosmic alignment, like how I met my husband or how a dear friend knew I was pregnant days before I physically was.

But I can say the best things in my life came out of centered, crystal-clear, crazy-happy pockets of time when fear was on a coffee break. That momentum of joy gave me the strength, right now, at thirty-six, to tackle my biggest roadblock, my biggest fear: the fear of abandonment or of becoming an outcast because of my artistic and personal beliefs.

I'm a quick learner. I put myself in high-stakes situations with aggressive quotas and often insanely tight deadlines. That's how I work. That's how I've come to create this manifesto. To some, it might seem pretty early in a person's cycle of life to write a book. At times, I feel like it has come too late. But at least it has come, now.

This is my change: this manifesto.

I invite you to be a part of my ensemble, to interact, create, and declare your own independence creatively.

SELF-OBSERVATION:
I'm The Manifesto. And You Are...?

How do you introduce yourself?

How do you define yourself?

Are you using what you love or what you hate to define yourself?

Is your image of yourself dependent on your relationship with others?

If so, who specifically?

Do you stand solid in who you are in this moment?

If not, where do you waiver?

What is standing in the way of you being what you truly want to be?

When was the last time you asked yourself what you truly wanted out of your life? Ask now.

How does it feel to ask yourself these questions?

AVOIDANCE DANCE

*"There are some moments
we can spend a whole lifetime avoiding.
Ironically these are the moments
in which the most freedom is bound up."
— Sara Nolan*

I've been avoiding this moment all my life: the moment of reckoning, owning who I am and what I want. I bobbed and weaved like a prizefighter to avoid getting slammed. As a dear friend (and Broadway vet) often reminded me, "The only way to get hit by a punch is to stand there and let it hit you." For me, a person secretly wishing for community and interdependency, the fear was simple: Show people who you are, speak your mind clearly, stand solid in who you are, and everyone you love WILL leave you. And that "truth punch" would knock me out cold.

So, starting very early in life, I made an art form out of deciphering people's actions in order to anticipate, please and, well, be perfect. Mind you, it was not *my perfect*. Where was the value in that when the grades, affection and jobs were in the hands of others? I was creating an avoidance dance. Complex choreography and interchangeable partners (teachers, family, friends, bosses), all with the same role: to show me I wasn't ready to step up yet and take the punch. Always teetering on the edge of who I really was. Two steps forward, one step back. I began relying on negative criticism and fear to motivate me. Only *there*, in reacting to negativity, was I finding momentum.

When I was in elementary school, I had a dynamic Russian ballet teacher, passionate in every sense of the word, yelling at us to strive harder, forcefully pointing out our flaws and failures. It was a huge motivator to do well. But the biggest motivator was what I noticed one day waiting for my turn across the floor.

Our teacher was fully engaged with those that were talented and/or skilled. But toward the others, he was deathly silent.

The Intensity of the Criticism = (Talent x Skill) ^{Effort}

In my pattern-focused mind, always looking for clues and subtext, his silence (and soon all silence) meant you had either zero talent or zero skill. And criticism as a form of attention blurred into the idea of criticism as a form of love or caring.

Let's look at that equation again:

$$\textit{The Intensity of the Love} = \textit{(Talent x Skill)}^{\textit{Effort}}$$

Striking a chord with anyone?

This desire for love, as I understood it then, became a primary motivator to encourage and seek out criticism from my teacher, my audience... anyone. It continued into my adult life, the encouragement-slap-down combo. I began to distrust people that didn't have cutting advice for what I needed to work on in my art and my life. There was always room for improvement, and never room for acceptance of me-right-now.

This was a dizzying dance that I was choreographing myself. It took so much effort to find others to show me who I was. There were so many dance partners that fell short of my need or were too much for me. It was me who needed to step up and learn a different dance:

Responsibility. Exploring the unknown. Ownership. Joy. Failing gloriously. Unparalleled success. Full awareness. Honest relationships. Unfettered creativity.

So... Now I am standing completely still. Looking myself dead in the eye. My breath is even and deep.

And with all the courage I can muster, I state, "Manifesto, lay one on me."

SELF-OBSERVATION:
Manifesto Mambo

What have you been avoiding?

Is it a scenario? A person? A responsibility?

What are your avoidance strategies?

How do you take criticism?

Do you rate your actions against those of others?

Do you rate your actions against your expectations of yourself or your current standards?

Is this scale made by you or inherited from someone?

Whom do you go to for criticism? Why this person?

Whom do you hate getting criticism from? If so, why?

How do you best process criticism?

Does criticism need to be given in a certain tone to be receivable?

Are some themes or topics off-limits for criticism?

What are you scared of hearing about yourself?

What are you ready to tackle and own about yourself?

What would help you to stand still and take on the world?

How does it feel to ask yourself these questions?

THE "WHAT IF?" DOORWAY

Imagine the following scene: You are standing in front of a life-size movie screen watching the fiction of your past, present and future run its course. I call it "fiction" because all memories warp over time, the past is subjective and the future is pure speculation. But if you hold up a small mirror, you'll see slight differences in your present self and the one on the movie screen. If you allow your ensemble to help hold a larger mirror, you'll see even more differences between your life now and your fictional version.

Self-observation has the same function as this mirror.

The next shift is important: it marks the difference between declaring independence and *being* independent. It is the creative act of allowing for the unknown.

With the help of your ensemble, make a small hole in that movie screen. Now rip it into a larger one until you've made a "What If?" doorway, an opening into conscious living.

What if I could hire myself, right now, for the job of my dreams?

What if I told my lover all my fears and we became even closer because of it?

What if money didn't exist?

What if I flipped my schedule to a five-day weekend and two-day week?

What if I packed what I needed, sold the rest, and moved to that far-off country?

What if I didn't have to ask anyone's permission to take a holiday?

"What if..." is a tried and true prompt for the creative arts. It's the giggle of imagination. And that creativity is a staple in successful people's lives.

Successful = Happy in your life choices

I've encountered successful people with all kinds of lives: entrepreneurs, stay-at-home parents, teachers, artists, students, and CEOs. It didn't matter if they were young or old, healthy or ill, rich or poor. They found freedom, whether momentary or life-long, inside creative, intentional choices sparked by—or inside of— the power of their ensemble. I've seen it with my own eyes in the creative process of our company.

Creativity is not just for the lucky ones. Creativity is not just for the 'talented' ones. Creativity is not locked up for only artists to use.

Creativity is our birthright—that's right, for all of us— in the form of play, resourcefulness, and imagination. It was the primary tool each one of us used to explore the world and our place in it as children. It is the work, the hard work, of children.

What, it doesn't *look like* children are "working" with all that chaos, fun, and giggling going on? That might be because we are all in desperate need of setting ourselves free of the current definition of "work." Immediately.

Work—even repetitive tasks that could feel meaningless or mind-numbing—can be an absolute blast, as long as it's on your terms.

Consider the repetitiveness of the process of learning how to eat by yourself. No wonder babies wear their food as much as they eat it.

"I'll try this spoon-contraption a few times, sure. You say it goes in my mouth, Mom? Okay. Ugh, that's frustrating. Whose bright idea was this? Oops, aaahhhh! To heck with this, oatmeal feels good on my face. Wonder if this spoon is really a catapult? Wait, I'm still hungry. Let's try again."

They're getting creative! They're learning on their terms.

To figure out what "your terms" are, you must ask yourself who you are, right now, without all this fear. (More on this in the next section.)

Consider this the opportunity to pause, reassess, and become your own personal revolutionary. The sharper the knife, the easier it'll be to cut that movie screen. Not ready to weld a knife, then get creative, a sharp wit or bent hairpin can work wonders.

The process starts with questions… and it will end with questions. Don't be afraid: questions are wonderful and full of potential. We will work on embracing the "What If?" with joy and vigor.

There is no blame here. There is no need for "Oh, if only I had…"

There is only what is possible now. Now, where you move forward through the "What-If?" doorway into uncharted territory.

SELF-OBSERVATION:
I'm Ready For My Close-Up, Mr. Manifesto

How is your day sculpted?

Who makes the decisions about what happens during your day?

Do you need to get parts of your day approved by others? If so, who?

What's a successful day for you?

Who measures your degree of success—you, or someone else?

Are there aspects of your life (past, present or future) that you've handed over, even in a small way, to someone else?

If so, what have you handed over, and to whom?

In exchange for what? Money? Security? Opportunity? Love? Acceptance?

How does it feel to ask yourself these questions?

ON YOUR TERMS

A friend was speaking to me about his feelings of being at the mercy of the next audition or of time running out on his health insurance coverage for his family. He was telling the shadowy side of the freelancer's story: "This is what they *don't* tell you about living life on your terms."

"But are you truly living life 'on your own terms' when you use phrases like 'at the mercy of'?" I asked him.

Then the penny dropped, and he had an insight into his "terms":

> **"I need to remind myself
> that having things 'on my terms'
> doesn't require a shrinking of reality,
> dreams, expectations and my world
> to better control it 'on my terms'."**

Absolutely!

Shrinking those dreams is *not* living on your terms, not really. It's living on your *fear's terms*.

Inside our ensemble, a digital forum of passionate freelancers with multiple perspectives, we helped my friend articulate and self observe his true issue. He was making a few fears into "Facts" (capitalized for their imperialism). For example the *One Way* he could keep his health insurance, the *Only Two Ways* he could get a job he wanted, the *No Way* he could provide for his family while doing what he loved.

He made supported self-observations about his assumptions, took ownership of his fears and hopes and became vulnerable enough to the Unknown to ask the ensemble some basic questions about his *actual* needs.

The ensemble offered collaborative leadership and divergent thinking from their own lived experiences, options that my friend was unaware of and stories of ultimately humorous failures. He could put his fears into perspective. He could even make art out of them.

This is where your ensemble comes into play. Other like-minded seekers, who, like you, also need to be creatively independent, will be there to acknowledge and support your revelations.

Your ensemble is a reminder that you're not out of your mind for wanting to live life on *your* terms—not someone else's terms, and certainly not fear's terms.

You're not crazy.

My friend was putting unbelievable pressure on himself based on his "movie screen" version of what a husband/ dad/provider/adult in his life situation *should* be doing right now. At any moment the Dad Police would take him downtown for even considering raising his insurance deductible to the bare-minimum, a.k.a. "hit by a bus" coverage. Or was that knock on the door the Phony Press coming to release world-wide the fact that he's been faking it with *no clue* about how to be a productive member of society? The pressure were paralyzing him making him feel "less than" for not having his act together. He was focusing on what he was doing *wrong* by not meeting other peoples' terms for success.

You're not "less than".

His ensemble helped refocus him creatively on his terms, as yours will do: what makes him happy? What are his true "necessities"? What does he bring to the table of life, and what does his ensemble brings to the table?

Creatively, we were leaning on a performance method for the imagination: the suspension of disbelief. This fairly well-known device allows the audience to step into the "what if's" of the work with more eagerness and faith in order to explore the unknown without being road-blocked by what they consider "possible.".

Funny side note, this phrase assumes that being in disbelief is our general customary state, thus theatre asks its audience to suspend their "natural" behavior for an hour or two. But think about it: We could easily say theatre requires "a heightened belief", so too will this manifesto (more on that later). But as Hamlet would say, "Ay, there's the rub!"

Thankfully, suspension of disbelief helped my friend hold back his fears for an hour or two in order to play in the "what if" of his own terms. *What if* he stopped answering phones for his insurance coverage and finished the play he's been writing *about* the insanity of answering phones? Yes, buddy, we all remember when you started the job as "research"... three years ago.

This is a journey, an adventure and it is never really over or resolved. But the more conscious you are, the more you inject play and vulnerability into it, the more you take the risks you need to take, the more wonderful the journey becomes...

Because it's on YOUR TERMS.

What are your terms? Have you asked yourself? Ask now.

And really listen. Write it down. Own it.

And... if only silence follows when you ask... if you have no idea where to start... Write that down: "I don't know, yet."

It's a start.

Only empty pockets have the room to be filled. Empty your head of other people's terms (or fear's terms). Leave room for you. You'll show up.

Appreciate the risk you're taking, the vulnerability of this step. It's a powerful one.

SELF-OBSERVATION:
Manifesto, It's Time to Come to Terms With...

Write your list of non-negotiable terms for living your life.

Write a list of 'If I won the lottery' terms.

Write a list of 'If time wasn't an issue' terms.

What terms from the 'If' lists can you put on your non-negotiable list?

What can you do, today, to step closer to those terms?

What is in your way?

How does it feel to imagine this kind of life?

Are you breathing deeply? Breathe. Observe the breath.

Now, scratch out the following from your lists:
~~If I won the lottery...~~
~~If time wasn't an issue...~~

Read the lists aloud, in a tone that suggests these are your new non-negotiables.

How does it feel to ask yourself these questions?

THE ACT OF DECLARING

We ALL can benefit from intentionally choosing our path, our ensemble, and our experiences. There is power in a well-chosen community or ensemble. There is support and joy in owning the personal responsibility as the creators of our experiences.

Declaring independence and embracing creativity allows us ALL to create vibrant life experiences.

This path, this energy, is contagious. This focus and intention has the power to extend beyond the moment we tap into, beyond the moment of creation and into unknown potential. The one thing in our way is our focus on FEAR.

These fears aren't on my hit list, anymore. In fact, they're no longer on *any* of my lists. This manifesto is a calling-out of these fears enabling me to make a 180° turn from their gaze. The fears on this list can and will watch my back as I dance excitedly away towards a freer me.

It was time to say good-bye to the fiction holding me back from saying: "I'm Jess Pillmore, a creatively independent person. Nice to meet you, World."

Before going any further, into what the world holds for those that are ready to claim their creative independence there's a crucial step: Own *your* list.

SELF-OBSERVATION:
Nothing To Fear, Manifesto, But...

Invite every life-limiting fear you have into the room. It's roll call time.

Observe your breath, body tension/ease and mental dialogue.

Try to make a declarative statement releasing yourself from one of those life-limiting fears.

How does it feel to make a declarative statement about yourself?

What is something you want to declare about yourself, but have not yet declared?

What is a life-limiting fear that you would like to declare independence from?

How does it feel to declare it now?

What kinds of self-declarations are easy for you? What are harder?

How does it feel to ask yourself these questions?

THE
ENSEMBLE

I Am

Because We Are

SINGING IN THE SHOWER

Your ensemble doesn't have to be large for it to be powerful and effective.

Imagine your idea is a song and your ensemble is the shower. Yes, that's what I said, stay with me, I'm gonna get all creative on ya.

You might have a quiet song at the beginning. Your voice might not have that much intention, commitment or playfulness behind it—yet. Remember, you're just starting out and rebuilding the confidence and vocal muscles to really play. That takes time and effort. Don't rush it or you'll get shampoo in your eyes.

Singing a song to a stadium of people takes a lot of intention, strength and passion. Without that it is hard to reach even the first row in a venue of thousands. People paid for a rock concert but now they're watching a mime act. Not good! And I dig mimes, but not when I paid to see U2.

But in the shower, that song, even if sung softly, will inevitably hit corners and heights you didn't think possible. There is a reason we all sound great in the shower. It is small, enclosed, intimate. The acoustics are wonderful. You sound vibrant as the notes bounce quickly back to you. You take risks, get silly and try on different sounds and styles. You can also quickly self-correct if you sound off. The feedback is almost instantaneous.

When your self-awareness grows, when your intention, commitment and play expands, so will your ensemble. Your song will start to require more space, more participation, more players. You won't be satisfied with just the rubber ducky's quiet approval. The walls of that tiny room will start to push back further and further until, perhaps, you are sending your ideas and voice out into the entire world. Clothing optional, no judgment here.

Build up your strength. Build up your vocal chords. Build up your playful nature. Build up your ensemble. Build up your intention and commitment to project outward.

Story goes, the first time Barbra Streisand sang for anyone else, it was only for two dear friends. She made them turn around and face the wall, so as not to see her embarrassment or fear. We all know how that turned out. Start small.

SELF-OBSERVATION:
Sing Out, Manifesto

What idea have you sent out into your ensemble?

What was the feedback?

How large was your ensemble?

How does it feel to present an idea to your ensemble?

Do you have to mentally prepare or do you feel comfortable riffing with the ensemble?

What is something you'd like to "sing" for the ensemble, but haven't yet?

What's holding you back?

What can you do, today, that would help you to present that idea?

How does it feel to ask yourself these questions?

FEEDBACK LOOP

If you are intentionally asking "Is this a ridiculous idea? Am I insane for thinking it would work?" Your feedback will be "Yes, this is a ridiculous idea and you're insane for thinking it could work."

Why is *this* the feedback? You *asked* for it!

We get defeating feedback because we've sent out defeatist questions or intentions. There's that fear instinct again saying "I told you this would put the boardroom to sleep. See?"

Our mind focuses on whatever it is told to hone in on. That's why you start to see your model car *everywhere* as soon as you buy it. Or how you "accidentally" hear your new love's name, when no one's saying it: "Oh did you say 'Look at this'? I thought you said, 'Look at Chris.'"

Why? Because you cued your brain to perceive it that way.

This is called *cognitive reframing*, the process by which we take in information and alter it to fit our needs or current understanding. We have an instinctual need to "find meaning" in what happens around us. We all act on it voluntarily or automatically. The road to creative independence involves being conscious about how you reframe.

Knowing all this, what does it say when we prepare ourselves for the worst? The worst kind of feedback or the worst outcomes in any given situation? We usually get just what we ask for. Oh life, you literalist, you! So why not prepare ourselves for the best?

Prepare for the best-case scenario where you *do* know what you're talking about, you *do* have people around who get the joke, and *are* enjoying what you have to offer.

Be clear with your intention. Be clear with how you want your work to expand in the world. Be vulnerable enough to put your true intentions out there.

Once you've done that, there's another critical step.

Understanding the feedback:

By consciously focusing your intention, you own the feedback you are asking for. You are no longer at the mercy of whoever is giving that feedback. You understand that you got the ball rolling. Allowing feedback to come to you and welcoming it with the purpose of making your work clearer is empowering.

But rejecting or blocking feedback is one heck of a wall to push against. Many times this reaction—amygdala alert!!—comes out of mistaking feedback about your work as feedback *about you personally*. Or mistaking feedback for *fact*, instead of *opinion*.

But if you can breathe when receiving feedback and observe your reactions to it, you can tap into a means for powerful steps forward.

<blockquote>
The goal isn't to be liked,
because, hopefully,
we already like ourselves.
The goal isn't to be validated,
because our life is already valid.
</blockquote>

The real goal is to commit to a path where it is valid to always explore, question and expand. The goal is to live in the now to the best of our ability, and be open to what we're *really* asking for.

SELF-OBSERVATION:
Manifesto Sound Check 1-2, 1-2

What type of feedback are you looking for?

How do you feel when you get positive feedback?

What is your first response?

How do you feel when you get negative feedback?

What is your first response?

Observe which motivates you into action more readily.

How do you choose whom to ask for feedback?

List the people you frequently ask for feedback.

How do you normally frame your request for feedback?

The next time you ask for feedback, observe your breath, the thoughts in your head, and how you are standing.

THE ENSEMBLE

These are all clues on what type of feedback you're *really* asking for.

Try not to judge your observations: aggressive, defeatist, hopeful, etc. Simply observe the ease or tension present in your body.

How does it feel to ask yourself these questions?

THE SUBTEXT DIET

We're an interdependent community. Our lives are intertwined in ways we can't comprehend. Take a look at one twelve-hour period of your life. How many people did you interact with? How many people did your actions affect in one way or another? How many objects that you used were made, delivered, or disposed of by others? I have a feeling that makes for a long cast list for your twelve-hour documentary.

With each person comes all their experience, hopes, fears—past, present, and future. With each person comes your experience, hopes, fears—past, present and future—that you imprint on them. Does that barista remind you of someone? Did your friend just say something your father always says? These are just a few examples of conscious connections your mind makes amidst hundreds of subconscious ones.

How do we see each person as they are in the moment, without all the confusing and misleading extra stuff? I recommend a communication cleanser I call The Subtext Diet.

It's an exercise in awareness, high expectations, and vulnerability. Our mind jumps to conclusions, makes "sense" out of a pregnant pause in the conversation, in order to scratch fear's itch. It is the fear of the unknown that demands answers, no matter if they are accurate answers.

The Subtext Diet came out of a time in my relationship with my husband when sleep deprivation was high and tolerance was low (combine a baby sleeping in his bed for the first time with a family relocation to a new state and grad school). My best friend suggested that whenever Chris and I talk, we take each other at our word. No more looking into what that sigh 'really meant' or hearing 'I'm not angry, just tired' and translating it into 'I'm not going to tell you I'm angry. Tired is an excuse.'

It was hard, shockingly hard. It took many reminders to keep us on the diet, but it was worth it making us stop fabricating problems where there weren't any or making tiny problems bigger. It also required us to say what we needed and felt, because we knew the other person was no longer looking between the lines. We had to step into our authentic self and speak up, even when that authentic self was sometimes needy and tired.

Going on the subtext diet doesn't make the skill perfect. Like self-observation, it issues a constant reminder to speak authentically. We have made the conscious choice to mean what we say and say what we mean.

Clear lines of communication are imperative for a healthy ensemble. Otherwise, things can slip through the cracks and fester, becoming larger than life.

Giving the ensemble your honest self and expecting that of them is a wonderful place to start. It is a grounded and fruitful foundation for establishing long-lasting and creative relationships.

Take a day, a week, a month to take people at their word. Set yourself up for the same challenge.

SELF-OBSERVATION:
Stop Looking for Trouble, Manifesto!

How long can you go without reading between the lines when someone speaks to you?

Try to double that span today.

Name someone whom you naturally take at his or her word. Why do you?

Name someone whose words you tend to attach subtext to. Why do you?

What makes you get the most nervous in conversation? Direct language? Silences? Persistent questions? Humor? Politeness?

What would happen if you took everyone at their word for 24-hours?

Try it for an hour.

Observe when your mind starts to add subtext, filling in the blanks.

Why is it doing this?

With whom in particular does your mind go on a subtext binge?

Does this happen more in a particular environment or situation?

How does it feel to address these questions?

AS ONE

Does every situation require a designated leader? I challenge that assumption: No.

There are times when the ensemble will feel as if there is no leader because the flow is so strong. A sense of interdependency, personal commitment, and clear intention will open the door to an amazing phenomenon, *As One*. The moment when the group doesn't ask or need a map or leader, they tap in as a collective to the group intelligence.

As One is the physical representation of the collective consciousness, a way to tangibly experience the power of energy, brain waves and universal creation of thought.

These group actions force us to explore and exercise tolerance. Everyone is, in essence, doing their own thing in their own way but *As One*. Choreographer Merce Cunningham, composer John Cage and visual artist Robert Rauschenberg did it for ten years creating individual pieces/compositions within a specified time frame and bringing them together *As One* only at the last moment.

Look through history and you can see waves of collective consciousness. Ever notice how movies tend to come in thematic waves (multiple natural disaster films, for example)? Big-budget movies take years to develop from the initial idea into the final product. Yet handfuls are released simultaneously that share a core theme.

At first, our company created exercises in *As One* to bond an ensemble. Now, these are foundational creation tools. Simple tasks were proposed: *Sit As One. Run onstage, look up and laugh As One.*

But unlike Collaborative Leadership where an individual takes the lead for any given action, these moments are initiated and committed to simultaneously by the entire group. But maybe you wonder: if there are no cues given, then how does it work?

When awareness is honed vulnerability, commitment, and play are accessed, and the group finds their way through a sixth sense. I would even venture to say that it is our fearful need to over plan that usually drowns out the conscious collective. We've trained our ears to respond more to the emergency siren than the almost silent breath of collective purpose.

The hardest part of working *As One* isn't actually accessing the unity, but accessing the trust. We have been trained for so long that in every situation there is a leader and a follower. But we lose spontaneity and a larger connection to community when we hold onto this model as the only way to work.

As One requires trust in the ensemble. *As One* requires trust in yourself. You will make the "right" choice: just commit and be aware.

SELF-OBSERVATION:
Create, Play, Connect AS ONE, Manifesto

When have you experienced a moment of *As One* in work or in everyday life?

Can you think of an example, outside your own personal experience, where you've noticed the collective consciousness at work? In nature, science, etc.?

How do you feel when discussing this idea?

See if you can, with your group, explore *As One.* Give yourself a simple task like *Clap once As One.* See what happens.

Did you rely on cues or a leader? If so, try again. Close your eyes if necessary.

How did that feel? Did you hesitate? Did you barrel forward?

When you achieved the "one clap *As One*" did you acknowledge it and stop, feeling *As One* that the task was accomplished? Or did your ensemble, so over-focused on being *As One,* not realize the goal was already achieved, and so kept clapping?

How does the group know when they've done the action *As One*?

How does it feel to ask yourself these questions?

A DIAMOND AND ITS VOLCANO

Working towards your authentic self requires the same heat, pressure, and concentration that make stunning and strong diamonds. Trying to generate sufficient conditions alone could take eons, but your ensemble can help you advance your personal independence with lightning speed, adding the necessary pressure and heat to solidify your idea. And then, like volcanoes launching diamonds, your ensemble can rocket you up to the light of day.

Over the years, I've witnessed people launch their personal freedom (their diamonds) into the light of day through low time, high risk, awareness, empathy, vulnerability, and play. Here's a poignant example that stays with me.

A group of teens, fourteen to eighteen year-olds, were writing, rehearsing and performing a play over five weeks. A bold task in this concentrated time frame—roughly sixty total rehearsal hours. Plus, they didn't know each other well, and their group was comprised of different grade levels, degrees of experience, body shapes, economic classes, sexes, and races.

Our company set up situations to help them find their unique strengths, to create their diamonds. Without words, we demonstrated a safe carry, a piggy-back ride. Everyone in the group repeated these movements, and then walked around the room, trading who carried and who was being carried.

Grabbing new partners, Chris and I moved on to other types of lifts: hip and over-the-shoulder. Murmurs, giggling, and some flat-out refusals showed that this exercise was challenging what the group *knew* was possible: "This boy's too scrawny to lift me!" "I'm big, so I'm better at lifting people." "Girls can't lift guys." All of these assumptions had turned into limiting beliefs. But we kept walking, never stopping the exercise because of someone's fear. Safely, we moved through the lifts, retraining the amygdala. We were *all* capable of doing these moves in our own way. Within minutes the air changed from, "You're hands-down crazy; I'm not doing that!" to "Quick, take a picture, I'm doing it!"

Then, the big test. Silently we gathered in a circle. Chris picked up a student and passed him around like a vertical stick, from one person to the next until the "floating student" came back to his original spot.

There was a shout of victory, of unified strength and of a true ensemble forming. But could we do this with everyone? The group energy see-sawed between hope and fear. This is where the inexplicable power of the ensemble kicked in. Silently, safely the group *as a whole* took on the challenge, even as individuals struggled to fully trust. The ensemble supported each student without one fall, without one person opting out of the exercise, without one injury.

At the end, when the turn came of a beautiful girl of 200+ pounds, we all paused. All day she had opted out of being carried. But here, completely vulnerable and brave, she looked to the person next to her in the circle and nodded. The little girl next to her, 100 pounds soaking wet, smiled broadly, excited by the responsibility, and began to float her around the circle without faltering.

How did they do it? Physics, weight sharing, trust, extra help from the ensemble, heightened awareness within the ensemble, the pure focus of "yes", and suspended disbelief. It all came into play.

The sound bursting from us as we cheered was that of a volcano erupting seventeen diamonds high into the air. Without the pressure, high-stakes, short amount of time, vulnerability, play, and ownership of the ensemble, these individual diamonds of freedom would not have been formed.

It's a fallacy that you need to know your ensemble for years before creating a productive bond. It can, and often does, take years *if* the pressure and stakes are low and vulnerability and trust is slow to develop, due to lack of ownership of the process. But, as was true for this dynamic group of teens, there are ways to expedite the process with explosive results.

You strengthen yourself and the ensemble by honoring your vulnerability.

It is the bravery of future leaders to say,
"This is worth doing,
but I can't do it without you."

SELF-OBSERVATION:
Manifestos Are a Girl's Best Friend

How do you empower the ensemble? And they, you?

THE ENSEMBLE

How did you support the ensemble? And they, you?

Describe a personal risk, large or small, that you took due to the support of your ensemble.

What types of support do you need within your ensemble?
Verbal? Physical? Emotional? Humorous? Critical?

How do you support your ensemble?
Do you provoke? Encourage? Shake it up? Comfort?

What is a risk that you would like to attempt with the help of your ensemble?

How can they support you in this risk-taking?

How does it feel to ask yourself these questions?

RHYTHMIC
REVOLUTION

I Am
Because We Are
The Change

BEATS TO MOVE YOU
Rhythms of a Revolution

This chapter explores a few key rhythms to try on in order to become creatively independent. I call these processes *rhythms* because we all have internal heartbeats organically driving us forward. Music accesses a primal motivation.

Music emotionally, physically and psychologically alters a current state.[*]

Dropping into a rhythm is like riding a river's current. You can't see the current, but you can feel it. It can exhaust you, if you swim against it. It can multiply your efforts, if you swim with it.

Slip in, experience the flow. Here are a few of the rhythms I remix with my arts education company. Let yourself move and be moved inside them. Explore. Gather an ensemble to explore with you. Keep breathing. It is amazing how the simplest action of a deep breath can help us process a moment.

---

[*] I've listed fun references in the back if you're curious.

RHYTHMIC REVOLUTION

*Vulnerability * Connection * Risk-Taking * Divergent Thinking * Awareness * Ownership * Play * Intention * Collaborative Leadership * Failing Gloriously * High-Stakes*

Your personal independence has many grooves. This global revolution has many flavors. Creative independence has the flair and diversity of an international music festival, spanning decades of great artists from diverse communities.

I've found these rhythms help access the authentic. I've seen them help even the shyest wallflower dance his way into the spotlight of what he can be.

Groove on each rhythm in the order I have laid out, or play them on shuffle. As long as you turn up the volume, move the furniture out of the way and get your sweat on.

Once you've explored them all, you can go back and choose which rhythms can best serve you now on your journey. Be mindful of the rhythms you choose; they serve you in different ways, at different times. Your heartbeat will align with it. Your speed will increase or decrease accordingly.

Get ready, it's powerful. First rhythm... Vulnerability.

RHYTHM: VULNERABILITY
I Dreamt I Went to Work Naked

I can't prove this will work. This manifesto. For me. For you. For how long.

I can't be 100% sure about anything except to say: "I am, right now, trying my best to joyfully stand in my current situation while leaning towards my potential. And yes, I'm sucking in my stomach. I'm naked and vulnerable, not insane."

I know in my full awareness that this book is necessary. I have to do this. And it's okay that I'm doing it in this way, to this audience, at this time, with this experience, in my voice.

I know I need to be vulnerable in order to be honest. I know I need to be vulnerable in order to evolve. I know I need to be vulnerable in order to connect to you, a perfect stranger, in this intimate and yet amazingly removed medium of print.

But knowing only gets me halfway there. There's a big difference between knowing and understanding. I can know something intellectually but not understand it internally, not yet act upon it instinctually. But knowing is a start. I knew the process of my arts education company was helping myself and others around me find their creative independence. Writing the book challenged that knowledge. It provoked me to step even deeper into my commitment to be creatively independent.

The physical creation of this book involved collaborations in research, development, feedback, editing and design. All of these steps took what I though I knew and played with it in the *real* world with others. Through this process I stepped into understanding. And that understanding will deepen as more people interact with this book, me and any works (lectures, workshops, future books) that are inspired from this creation.

Each step of the process, I thought I knew what it felt like to be vulnerable, naked. And yet, each subsequent step gave more opportunities to expose more. Some steps exposed parts of me that were hiding whether out of fear or shame. Other steps allowed me to let go of stories, relationships, processes and assumptions that had been weighing me down. Just ask my editor. A virtual stranger who couldn't pick me out of a crowd (of two) went through my last draft and gave me opportunity after opportunity to reveal more.

Vulnerability is a cycle. If we can breathe deep during the first millisecond of shock when the cold air hits our skin and observe without judgment, then we can acclimate to that particular vulnerable act. Think about it: at one time showing one's ankles was risqué and now there are nude beaches. It's all relative and a matter of degree.

I am standing at work naked. Fully awake. I wonder what vulnerable dream I'll have next?

SELF-OBSERVATION:
Peek-a-Boo, Manifesto Sees You

What is vulnerability to you?

Did you experience an opportunity to be vulnerable recently?

Did you take the risk or not?

Why?

What was the outcome?

What goes through your mind when you feel vulnerable?

How does your body react to being vulnerable?

Have you ever experienced a positive outcome from being vulnerable?

If so, what happened?

Try something that makes you vulnerable in front of your ensemble.

Observe your breath. Fear often makes it very shallow or held.

Try breathing deeply.

Try expanding in that breath.

You have the potential for growth with each vulnerable act.

How does it feel to ask yourself these questions?

RHYTHM: CONNECTION
Interdependent Living

The act of connecting is powerful. So powerful, in fact, that its polar opposite is shame.

In Brené Brown's 2010 TED talk *The Power of Vulnerability*, she defines shame as *"the fear of disconnection: Is there something about me that if other people know it or see it... I won't be worthy of connection?"*

Life-Limiting Fear.

Becoming independent of this fear requires active and creative connection to yourself and the world around you.

Connection redistributes the weight that you thought you had to carry alone evenly among the members of your ensemble, so that the journey is possible and even enjoyable.

Yes, it's all *your* furniture and belongings you carry-- but does that mean you have to lug your couch up three flights of stairs *alone* on moving day? Who are you, Sisyphus? He was condemned to push that rock up hill, all day, forever. But for the price of a few pizzas and an understanding about reciprocity down the line, you can have an enjoyable moving day with your ensemble...

That is, if you connect.

Mind you, some connections are complicated. Just like moving that couch upstairs with a few friends shouldering the load, connection requires degrees of coordination, trust, timing, listening, responding, patience, and empathy. But that complex negotiation is well worth it because connections open pathways for electrical currents to run through you and your ensemble. These currents carry ideas, inspiration, momentum, motivation, information, questions, and more.

Other connections can be as simple as looking someone in the eye.

They can be as simple as mentally putting yourself in someone else's shoes. It's as simple as taking a deep breath all the way down to your toes. It's as simple as acknowledging another person waiting in line with you.

By "simple", I really mean "uncomplicated." *Simple* does not mean *easy*. The ease comes with practice, the repetition that forms habit.

Connection is contagious. Connection creates momentum. Connection grows exponentially.

What stops you from connecting? What shames you?

You have *nothing* to be ashamed of.

That is: There is nothing you have done that bars you from looking another person in the eye, or empathizing, or breathing deeply. It's risky, yes, but it's a life-evolving risk.

We think we're protecting ourselves with shame, when the more powerful protection comes from connection. Start easy. Build up.

Retrain your brain and flip the shame. You don't need it anymore.

SELF-OBSERVATION:
M.A.N.I.F.E.S.T.O., Connecting the Dots

How do you connect with people on a daily basis?

How does it feel to connect?

When have you wanted to connect but didn't? Why?

Can you feel that resistance in your body—and if so, where?

When have you taken a risk, however small or large, and connected with someone?

What was the outcome of that risk-taking?

How did you feel after you made that connection?

The next time you have a moment when connection with someone is possible, observe your breath, mental chatter, and body tension/ease.

How does it feel to ask yourself these questions?

RHYTHM: RISK-TAKING
The "Gulp" Moment

Risk is attached to danger. In these potentially dangerous moments, your amygdala is not only on call, it is probably grabbing you by the collar and yanking you backwards with extreme force.

But danger is relative. Risk is therefore also relative. What was risky for you at ten years-old might feel effortless now. And the reverse is true. Imagine a room of business people asked to play a game of tag. Risky business for them now. Why the difference?

Risk is attached to danger. But danger does not always equal *death*. Only life-or-death danger should engage the amygdala. We must retrain it to distinguish between life-endangering risk and life-evolving risk.

Life-evolving risks can include:

* Speaking in front of a crowd.
* Saying "I don't know" to your boss, your child, your students, your ensemble, yourself.
* Taking or relinquishing the lead.
* Climbing on top of a pyramid of five people you've just met.

* Checking your email only once a day.
* Loving someone unconditionally.
* Choosing the unbeaten path.

The dangers attached to these types of risks can be scary, the outcomes unknown. These risks force you to be vulnerable for a moment, a month, a lifetime. These risks take you out of your comfort zone, your habits and what you think you know to be true.

My risk was admitting I had a strong opinion on this subject of independence.

My risk was turning that opinion into absolutes.

My risk was then publishing the manifesto as book and not an academic paper.

My next risk: standing behind it, come what may, AND allowing myself to be changed by how the ensemble interprets the work and the words.

Balance out the tiny risks with the massive ones. We get different energies and momentums from each.

The fear response to risk is programmed to feel absolute, eliciting a black-or-white, peril-or-peace response. When its secret service shouts "Code Red", I respond immediately. There's a reason fight-or-flight works and I'm very appreciative!

But life-evolving risks involve infinite grey areas. Wondering whether to call that high-profile artist and pitch a collaborative project is not the same as assessing the thickness of the ice before walking across a frozen river.

Track when you experience fight-or-flight fear responses to what are really grey-area risks. Go out and play in the grey. It can be as cool as the shade or as brilliant as silver. Grey gets a bad rap. Take a risk.

SELF-OBSERVATION:
Manifesto, A Game of Risk

What do you consider to be a risk right now?

Is it physical, emotional, occupational?

If success was guaranteed, what are a few risks you would take?

Is there something you do naturally without fear that others in your ensemble consider a risk?

Did you take an intentional risk today, on any scale?

If so, observe how it felt to make the commitment to that intentional risk.

Did it still feel like it had been a risk afterwards?

Is it harder to take a risk alone or in front of certain people?

How does it feel to ask yourself these questions?

RHYTHM: DIVERGENT THINKING
School Got It Wrong

Well, it's not that school got it wrong, they got exactly what they wanted—trained industrial workers.

For years, we've been trained to search for the correct answer. Education is a race to the *one* correct answer. And whether you can offer that *one correct answer* on this test, on these pop quizzes, to the boss's question, determines your future life path.... Ugh.

There is no correct answer.
That is, there is no *one* correct answer.

Take this for example: 1+1=3. Correct or wrong?

Sure, in basic arithmetic, it's wrong because 1+1=2 (always).

BUT...

In Biology, 1 female + 1 male = 3 (potential) family members.

In English, "one plus one = three"... words, that is.

What if there are no correct answer for a single question, only appropriate answers for questions in their given contexts?

The more we exercise our minds and our creativity and release our assumptions, the more easily we can solve the really difficult questions, the ones that can't be figured out by rote learning.

Divergent thinking works on the exact opposite premise of the *one answer* mindset. It challenges us to keep going, to keep creating new possible avenues for answers within the constructs of the question. To push beyond the single-thought stream, we need to borrow the concept of aggressive quotas.

Aggressive quotas, commonly used as motivators for sales teams, are a generative tool which energetically up the ante on results. These quotas demand a high output, which forces you to go beyond a knee-jerk, end-of-the-story answer, and truly push into the realm of "What if?"

Aggressive quotas test your creativity, stamina and playfulness. To push your thinking, you internalize that personal trainer who says, "Five more and you're done! 5-4-3-2-- No, let's do ten more! Then you're done! 10-9-8-7- Oh, you're looking great; let's go out with a bang-- with fifty more!"

The power combination of divergent thinking and aggressive quotas helps you push aside assumptions about a given task or question—which tend to deaden outcomes, anyway—in favor of exercising your highly-generative imagination with large quantity expectations.

Playing with never-ending "What if's?" is joy run amuck. And your fear is that annoying neighbor next door calling the Assumption Police just when the party gets going. Assumptions hold back progress and evolution in almost any domain. If you let them take over, they become tall walls which are camoflauged to *look* like your life but which are actually blocks keeping you from the palace of the unknown. And the unknown, the "impossible", is where your creative independence lives.

Let's try an aggressive quota and divergent thinking exercise: Let's say you have $20 and twelve-hours in New York City. Come up with 50 (yes, *five-zero*) ways to spend your day on the town. Then reflect on the process through which you generated your responses:

* How many options did you come up with before your thinking slowed down?
* How many of these response feel standard fare?
* Could you jump-start yourself into a new avenue of thinking?
* What assumptions were you making in this scenario?
* How many options did you come up with before you quit?
* How many of your options made you laugh out loud when you reread them, due to their pure ridiculousness?

* Did any options on the lists of your ensemble members cause you to respond, "Wait, was that *allowed*?"

You'll find that a process that at first feels like "more work than necessary" can actually become exhilarating, hilarious and insightful. Imagination does not live in the realm of efficiency. It thrives in the land of "Yes, *and...*", This phrase is a staple of theatre improvisation used to encourage more options within your generative process. Give me *more* worlds to explore, not *fewer*!

What if...? (And there is that phrase again!) What if the point of education was to teach us to shirk the one-answer tyranny in order to search for the next, ever-deeper questions? We work with whatever question is currently before us rigorously and relentlessly. This is a chance to consider multiple possibilities while utilizing intelligent research, experiential learning and play to dive into the deep end of the unknown.

This ripple is never-ending.

Education and exploration is—or ought to be—never-ending.

And it can and should be: that's where joy and uncharted lands lie.

And *that's* what school got wrong. Training us all, even those inside who perpetuate the system, that there is an *end* to education, i.e. when I get the correct answer, I can move on. This is a linear story and a finite one. Not to mention mind-numbingly boring.

According to "one answer only" thinking, Shakespeare's famous play of one man searching for the meaning of life would end rather quickly: "To be or not to be, that is the question":
a) *To be.* Hamlet's quest is done. Play over.
b) *Not to be.* Hamlet kills himself right then and there. Play over.

Shakespeare by Scantron? It's coming, and faster than you think if we keep marching to the One Answer drum beat. But life is too expansive to be shoved into an efficiency-driven grading tool like the Scantron bubble sheet.

And it's already slipping into our daily life. Think of how often we say, "What will I have for breakfast? A. cereal, B. coffee only, C. fruit, D. toast." Life is made up of more than three-four choices per question, as opposed to the auto-pilot, single answer, quick-let's-get-it-over-with reaction. Hopefully, this book will encourage you to answer that question with other questions to get to your unique answer.

"What will I have for breakfast?"

What do I feel like? What is in the fridge? What haven't I had in a while? Am I feeling adventurous? What do I need for the day I've got ahead of me?

Here are the biggest traps of "one answer" education: it promotes boredom, closed thinking and impatience. We are creatures driven to explore instinctually, playfully. But when "right or wrong", "yes or no" constricts the natural reaches of our process, we suppress that instinct.

Take these two scenarios:

First, look at children who can play with an empty cardboard refrigerator box for hours, days, weeks. What a child can do with this malleable object is endless: it comes without rules for usage. You can hardly separate the child from the box, it is so deeply connected to the imaginary world.

These same children, however, can "figure out" in minutes the toy that *beeps!* when a button is pressed; the child gets bored and throws it in a pile somewhere. Only occasionally does the child pick it back up, pressing the buttons to make sure it still *beeps*—hey, the universe is sometimes predictable. *Done, got it.*

That's a "one answer" beeping toy, as opposed to the "divergent thinking" refrigerator box—by which I mean, castle, house, rocket ship, boat, robot, cave, dinosaur, television, time machine, sled...

Education is an organic and infinite process.

When I find answers, I can move through, move in, and move with the information.

Information that challenges and influences a bigger—or the biggest?—question addresses Hamlet's agony directly, and appropriately, with another question:

Who am I and how do I want to live my life?

SELF-OBSERVATION:
100 Uses for this Manifesto. Go!

When you're trying to solve a problem, how do you know when you've hit on the (right) solution?

Do you think each question or problem has (only) one correct answer or solution?

If so, how does it feel to operate according to this model?

Who taught you how to approach questions?

What is your signal to stop generating solutions or potential answers?

How do you react to situations that cannot be resolved with a single answer?

Are you comfortable coming up with multiple answers?

List scenarios that encourage divergent thinking.

List scenarios that repress divergent thinking.

How does it feel to ask yourself these questions?

RHYTHM: AWARENESS
More Gifts Than We Know

We constantly use our capacity for awareness—consciously or otherwise—to assess the conditions of our inner and outer environment. Awareness helps us answer questions like:

Do I need to eat?

What's going on in my mind?

Who's standing close to me?

Did I feel how the room shifted when I spoke?

In this crowded store, which person knows if this shirt is included in today's sale?

Awareness is invaluable for averting the dangers—high and low stakes—of a crowded world. Have you ever stood in line, only to have Mr. Unaware in front of you back up as if he was the only one in the room? Luckily, you *were* aware of your physical existence, and of the existence(s) of the people behind you, and stepped the to side. Squished toes averted. Thanks, Awareness!

Awareness is a key to living a conscious life. And those who fascinate us most with their talents and creative lives have often made an art form of awareness: they are plugged into who they are, what drives them, and what they want. I would even go so far as to say refined awareness, in its many forms, might be what we are actually calling *talent*.

Talent is defined as a natural aptitude or skill. We have mystified that label just as we have the label "creative", as if it were reserved for a select few, not for all of us. But if we look at the many levels of awareness each of us can access, we might be able to find the natural root of these "mystical" talents.

Awareness, like a heartbeat, is key to every other rhythm in this book. Without it, there is no way to know what you are bringing to the table. Awareness gives you the ability to access your skills and natural tendencies for being creatively independent. Once you start to observe and claim ownership of this awareness, you can also begin to understand how you contribute to your ensemble.

Remember, any ensemble is a blend of the varied layers of awareness in each individual, and the *As One* awareness of the collective.

Awareness has multiple layers. Each of us can access these layers with greater or lesser dexterity. For fun, here are some Awareness Bingo cards for you and your ensemble. As you go through the list below, mark the ones you access on a daily basis. Don't forget, the first one to make a line shouts *Bingo*!:

RHYTHMIC REVOLUTION

AWARENESS
BINGO

COVERT AWARENESS	TIME AWARENESS	BASIC AWARENESS	LOCATION AWARENESS	GROUP STATUS AWARENESS
BASIC AWARENESS	SELF-AWARENESS	HIGHER AWARENESS	CONTEXT AWARENESS	SPATIAL AWARENESS
GROUP STATUS AWARENSS	LOCATION AWARENESS	FREE	TIME AWARENESS	COVERT AWARENESS
SPATIAL AWARENESS	BASIC AWARENESS	CONTEXT AWARENESS	HIGHER AWARENESS	SELF-AWARENESS
TIME AWARENESS	COVERT AWARENESS	LOCATION AWARENESS	BASIC AWARENESS	CONTEXT AWARENESS

Basic Awareness is the bare minimum we need for survival.

Self-Awareness involves deeper cognition, introspection, and a stronger distinction between yourself and the outside world. In child-development, the mirror test classically illustrates the onset of this type of awareness. Lipstick is put on a baby's forehead and he is held in front of a mirror. Before self-awareness kicks in, the baby will try to touch the lipstick mark on the reflection. When the higher cortical functions that contribute to self-awareness have developed, the baby will rub the lipstick off of his own forehead after seeing it in the mirror.

Spatial Awareness, what I call "I'm walkin' here!" awareness, is an understanding of the negative and positive space around you. It helps you avoid tripping over your own feet or other people's, and colliding with taxicabs.

Covert Awareness is when you know something without knowing how you know it. This occurs in blindsight, déjà vu, intuition, and post-hypnotic states.

Location Awareness is knowing where you stand, literally. If you've ever taken a ride in an underground subway (disorientation), exited on ground level, and in a heartbeat known in which direction—north, south, east, or west—you needed to start walking (orientation), then you've tapped into location awareness.

Context Awareness concerns how communities form bonds based on shared context or theme rather than based exclusively on common location. Examples of context awareness in action are the "small societies" you find in elderly communities or Silicon Valley.

Time Awareness is the internal clock that *never* loses the time. A life-saver awareness for the TED talker or stand-up comedian. It is good to intentionally block out this awareness when standing in line at the DMV or visiting your in-laws.

Group Status Awareness hones in on and identifies the hierarchy of a room or community. Perfect for those cocktail *meet-and-greets* with potential funders.

Higher Awareness involves a deeper understanding of that which is beyond the physical world, whether that involves energy or spirituality. It is an internal tuning fork to discover the vibrations connecting the room, ensemble, community and world.

And this is just the tip of the iceberg. I'm still waiting to discover the *Awareness Awareness*, or the ability to sense the many forms of awareness within a society or an individual. Is that what makes people wonderful teachers and coaches? I'll work on conjuring it.

Bingo, anyone?

When exploring the types of awareness active in yourself, try to look at it from two angles: a process of ownership and of discovery.

Asking "What am I aware *of*—" can also lead you to answer the question: "What *talents* do I have?"

For example, I can always sense when someone is standing close to me. I used to think I was *sensitive* or *uncomfortable* in crowds. This might be true—but my *talent* is also that I have a heightened level of spatial awareness. What I do with that gift is based on my ownership of it and commitment to strengthen it. Great spatial awareness enables me to safely design and teach physical theatre techniques in conference rooms of 150+ participants who are jumping, lifting, and climbing on each other.

A teaching artist watched one of these workshops and later remarked, "You can't have that many people on their feet working without it becoming dangerously chaotic." I replied, "Maybe *you* can't—or wouldn't want to—but you just watched Chris and I do that very thing for two hours. And you saw the response: joy, energy, ownership, and students coming back for the next workshop with more friends *and* their teachers in tow. It's how we teach because it's what we do."

Chris and I both have developed our awareness in spatial relationships, safety (physical and emotional), risk assessment, tension and play. These forms of awareness have a protective as well as expressive function; with them, we assess, consciously and subconsciously, how to keep others safe, while allowing them to experience open joy in their own personal risk. That's awareness.

When you get stumped trying to assess your awareness strengths, go the reverse route. Look back at the list of the different types of awareness. Notice which ones intrigue you, or remind you of the talents of someone in your ensemble, or sound similar to your own (undiscovered) *talents*.

For example, until researching this book, I was unaware (ha-ha!) of my facility for Group Status Awareness. When I looked more deeply at its definition, I saw, "That's me!" I have a knack for quickly assessing the status order of an ensemble: the leader, the follower, the middle man, etc. I used to assume that came from the theatre director in me looking for a story—now I realize it is a *talent* for a particular mode of perception.

Exploring your awareness and natural tendencies can give rise to *"chicken-or-the-egg?"* scenarios. Am I a director/choreographer because of my natural abilities in Spatial and Group Status Awareness? Or have those aspects of awareness grown more prominent because of my creative work as a director/choreographer? Probably a little of both.

Becoming aware of what you are aware of can feel circular, but add in some Ownership (coming up next) and this "circle" can serve to spiral you towards creative independence.

SELF-OBSERVATION:
Open Your Eyes, Manifesto, You're Aware Now

Which types of awareness are strong in you?

Which types of awareness are weaker in you?

Which ones are completely new to you as concepts?

Which ones could help you live more independently?

How do you use or play with the various types of awareness every day?

How do you imagine you could strengthen your awareness across all categories?

How does it feel when testing out a new awareness?

How does it affect your breathing, stance, body tension and focus?

What new awareness will you try today? How?

How does it feel to ask yourself these questions?

RHYTHM: OWNERSHIP
Please Sign Here For Your Stuff

Ownership. This can be complicated to sort out in an interdependent world. What truly is mine? What truly is yours?

When we conceive of "ownership", we usually mean it in the material sense of owning "things." But for our purposes, I'd like you to consider a more fundamental ownership: owning one's thoughts, feelings and actions.

This is your life and the buck absolutely can stop here. You have the power to stand in this moment and own your thoughts, feelings, actions and reactions. This is a form of wealth that never runs out.

A psychiatrist explained the relationship between ownership and awareness to me in terms of his work. Clients come in with pounding headaches and ask him to stop the pain. He tells them, "Stop hitting yourself in the head with a hammer. That would help." And they ask, "What hammer?" His job is to help them become aware of—and own—their hammers.

We need to figure out what *we* are responsible for, what we need to own about ourselves, to live the way we would wish. Dissatisfied with your situation? How often do we defer responsibility for this—and for our lives at large—to someone else? Our boss, teacher, doctor, parent, spouse? We tacitly allow them to create our reality for us, or to affect it disproportionately, because we have not yet accepted ownership of our actions, thoughts, and feelings.

But you can start to claim ownership with two simple questions: "What am *I* aware of?" and "*How* am I aware of it?"

Your answers are your property—they belong to you, and they are also where your independence lives. You alone could write a dissertation on the results of this inquiry. It's what makes you *YOU*. Own it.

The information you gather through your personal awareness capacity sculpts how you perceive *everything* around you.

Look at all how many "you's" are in the previous sentence. It's all *you*. Underline them. Highlight them. Circle them. Do what you have to do to take full ownership of the fact that this is *your reality*.

Ownership also allows you to accept yourself. Try looking at your natural abilities in a fresh light. These abilities can be anything that you *own* about yourself: are you an early riser, chatty, experimental cooker, sensitive listener, able to strike up a conversation with anyone, etc? The list can (and hopefully does) go on and on.

Take nothing for granted. Just because a quality or skill is instinctual to you does not mean it is a given for others. This is a step towards seeing ourselves not as products on an assembly line aiming towards average "perfection" but instead unique, flawed and irreplicable* pieces of art. I use to think that everyone, if given the option, would chose to find the most efficient way of completing any task, just because it was a natural impulse for me. Not so.

(*Side Note: Did you know there's no actual antonym to "replicable"? Really? Has the industrial era dug in to our culture that far? Stops now. Irreplicable, there it is. Let's embrace that which cannot be replicated.)

Even 'flaws' need to be owned in order to become assets. Broadway director/choreographer Bob Fosse created a distinctive style of dance from explicitly owning his "flaws" and consciously turning them into his art: bad posture, awful turnout, and premature balding. Not only did he own these traits, but he amplified them, creating a signature that even included the 'dark side' of sexuality. His unusual angles, curves, and sly hat-work not only transformed his supposed flaws into his creative independence, but earned him Tony, Emmy, and Oscar Awards.

You are a complicated being of infinite abilities, hopes, accomplishments and potential. Value yourself for what you are inherently capable of. Don't be indebted to someone else's version of you. Own your own thoughts, feelings and actions. Good, bad and complicated, they are yours (and will be, whether you own them or not). So why not let your full self be what sets you free?

If you can own the hammer in your hand—and not hit yourself with it impulsively—the next steps fall into place.

SELF-OBSERVATION:
"This Manifesto Belongs to _____."

What do you own about yourself?

What do you have a hard time owning about yourself?

Name something you can do, today, that would help you own one of those 'hard to own' traits.

When is ownership easy for you? In what situation(s), or around which people?

When is ownership difficult?

Do you try to own more or less than you are actually responsible for in a group situation?

If so, what? Why?

How does it feel to ask yourself these questions?

RHYTHM: PLAY
The Work of Children

Play is the work of children. It is how they explore the world and their place in it. And children work hard. A three-year-old's brain is twice as active as an adult's.

Play allows them to learn through modeling, role-playing, exploration and challenging status quo. Why do you think a toddler's "Why?" loop drives adults crazy? Because, at some point, the toddler hits what we really don't know or can't justify intelligently.

But instead of playfully investigating the answer, we usually shut it down with a final "because I said so!" or "because we *just do!*" Body language shows you a lot in this scenario, too. The child's "why" is open-ended and liquid, whereas the adult's "because" is a wall, rigid and closed.

Play also makes some pretty difficult things fun—like, say, mastering motor skills, language, gravity and emotions—adding buoyancy and joy. To get to mastery, these lessons require excessive repetition, which would become mind-numbing without the majority being experienced as play.

So, here's a thought: let's replace the word 'work' with 'play.' See how long you can do that in a day.

"See you honey, I've got to go *play* at the office."

"Oh Max, can you hand me some of those papers over there? Thanks, I'm *playing* with them."

"Got a problem with that theory, Linda? Well, let's hunker down and *play* it out."

Can it be that easy? YES!
Are you going to sound crazy? PROBABLY!
Do you care?
Think about it.

REMEMBER:
Feeling ridiculous and vulnerable
is the landmark for being on new ground.
And if you're on new ground,
then you're on the cutting edge.
You're a front-runner.

So, stay on your toes because…

TAG. YOU'RE IT!

SELF-OBSERVATION:
Tag + Manifesto = A Creative Revolution

What are some of your daily activities that feel far removed from play?

How could you, today, make them more playful?

When you see others playing, at any age, how does that make you feel?

How would you describe 'being playful'?

Where is play activated in your body? For example, do you start to bounce a little or smile? Do your hands get energized with wiggling fingers?

If you had a free thirty-minutes today for play *only*, how would you spend it?

Who embodies playfulness to you?

Who or what inspires playfulness in you?

What helps you become playful?

How does it feel to ask yourself these questions?

RHYTHM: INTENTION
Get the Keys

Intention...

Let's do some experiential learning first to reveal the potency of intention, then we will look at *why*. Chris and I have found that intention is also a visceral rhythm.

This next exercise is a staple for *Creatively Independent* because it has proven time and again to open a whole can of beans for... anyone. This exercise, "Get the Keys", reveals many aspects of our inner process, even beyond what we consciously intend. Try this with your ensemble, to learn about the relationship between intention, action and achieving goals.

GET THE KEYS:

* Put your keys (or shoe or a paper with your biggest dream written on it) on the floor at the edge of the room.
* Walk to the opposite side of the room to start.
* Turn to face the keys.
* Look at the keys. Really see them.
* Breathe them in.

* Now, close your eyes.
* Can you see the keys in your mind's eye?
* You get ONE GRAB. No sliding around, hunting, and pecking. One grab.
* Keep your eyes closed.
* Go get the keys!
* Stand up. Open your eyes.
* Breathe in your success or failure.

Talk about your experience with the group. How strongly did you want the keys? What went through your head or your body when you made that one grab? What was it like to succeed or fail in front of your ensemble?

It's a great lesson in experiencing the glorious consequences of vulnerability. For those watching you, it's palpable how having a clear, strong intention exerts a magnetic force on the journey.

The reaction of the ensemble to you is in direct proportion to your investment in the process. We (the ensemble) care about the person who *has* to get those keys, who is as motivated as if his or her life depended on it.

It's difficult for us to watch the person who's already given up in advance, who doesn't care right from the beginning, or accepts defeat along the way.

There are all kinds of inner-dialogues that accompany this task.

One kind is an act of self-protection, telling yourself, "It's okay if I don't get the keys. It's just a silly game and they're *only* keys after all" This thought instantly makes the effort and action of finding your keys pointless, even if you actually achieve your goal.

I've seen it in action a thousand times: The outcome, whether you get the keys or not, isn't actually the riveting part of the journey. What draws us in, both the participant and the audience, is the strength and quality of your intention.

For this to work, for this to be magnetic, you *have* to care. If you care, we care. And that care only grows exponentially as you proceed. You are suddenly in a field of support of your own making. This feedback loop of forward-leaning encouragement is due *exclusively* to your initial commitment to a positive unwavering intention.

When your intention is clear and strong, there is a bright spotlight on your goal and we all see it. You can feel it (the "keys", the goal) with your eyes closed, calling you from across a large room. I've even seen this done even across large football fields. Witnessing someone act with profoundly clear and committed intention is, hands-down, jaw-dropping.

We see this in both beautiful and horrific events in our world. This section focuses specifically on the act of committing. But know that the other sections in the book help you clarify what your "keys" are, in the big picture. It is the wish of this Manifesto that *what* you commit to is to be engaged in creative, community-focused and playful life choices based in hope not fear. Remember: actions motivated by fear bring only more fear.

The power of clear intention is intense. There's no "kinda-sorta-maybe" with clear intention.

What are your "keys" in life?

Can you see them now, with your mind's eye? Breathe them in. See yourself grabbing them. Make a connection to them. Now, go get them, with one decisive grab.

SELF-OBSERVATION:
Use the Force, Manifesto

Where does desire live in your body?

How does wanting something change your breathing? Your focus?

How does it feel to want something with all your heart?

What is something that you want, but have been afraid to admit how much?

What's holding you back from getting that one thing with ONE GRAB?

What does it feel like to want something, go for it and then fail?

Visualize yourself walking directly to what you want and getting it. How does that feel?

How does it feel to ask yourself these questions?

RHYTHM: COLLABORATIVE LEADERSHIP
Are You A Leader or A Follower?

You're both.

A creatively independent person is both leader and follower depending on the situation. You are teacher and student, boss and employee... you and the ensemble will ask for whatever role is needed in any given moment.

A flock of birds alters leaders without board meetings or memos. The elements of nature take their turns reshaping the globe. We can do the same. We just have to commit to two things: know what we personally offer the ensemble (see *Ownership*) and have the sensitivity to know what the moment needs (see *Awareness*).

Imagine you're in a clump of people, a tight ensemble, all standing close enough to touch. You happen to be in front, leading. You and the ensemble start walking. You encounter a wall, but you don't walk into it, right? No, you turn to face the open space, and the ensemble follows. But now, someone new is in front. This person has become the leader. The change happened naturally because of how all of you organically responded to your environment.

You have just naturally—without need for voting, negotiations or blueprints—played in the world of collaborative leadership.

The rhythm of collaborative leadership is a remix.
It is a deftly interwoven groove of play, intention, ownership, awareness and commitment.

I used to think I had to stand behind the best person in the room and attempt to "steal" everything that person knew, modeling myself in that light. This was bold advice given to me by a passionate teacher. And, in a way, he was absolutely right.

But in collaborative leadership, as I learned experientially over the years, everyone is the best at whatever he or she *understands*. What I *understand* is tapped in to what I am *aware of*, what I can see, feel, and (sometimes) anticipate. This is the horizon on which I am focused.

Sometimes, I'm *not* the one who can see, understand, or anticipate what's ahead. But I can feel my intention and the ensemble's physical and intentional presence. And with that understanding of collaborative leadership, engaging trust, connection and awareness, we run together at break-neck speed towards the horizon.

If you feel the wind shift, and the path opens up so you can see clearer skies ahead... take the lead.

Try it. It's fun.

SELF-OBSERVATION:
"Mom, Manifesto's Playing in Traffic Again"

Which role do you tend to play, leader, or follower?

Is your role consistent or does it depend on the dynamics of the group or situation?

If it's changeable, get specific about the situations in which you feel comfortable taking the role of leader and those in which you take the role of follower.

How does it feel when that role isn't available to you?

Can you recall recent circumstances where you had to impromptu lead? If so, how did that turn out?

How did it feel, physically, mentally, and emotionally?

Can you recall recent circumstances where you had to follow someone you weren't comfortable following?

How did that turn out?

How did it feel, physically, mentally and emotionally?

How does it feel to ask yourself these questions?

RHYTHM: FAILING GLORIOUSLY
The Dreaded "F" Word

"Failure" is such a dreaded word, for most. We were trained in school to avoid the big scarlet "F" at all costs. Fear (another F-word) is connected so tightly to failure that the potential for failure might in fact be *exactly* like a ravenous lion lurking in the bushes to our amygdala.

But it's not. Not really.

Failure to distinguish an edible berry from a poisonous one is *amygdala* territory. Failure to embrace the risk of recording your original song instead of a cover everyone knows is *independence* territory.

Failure is inevitable. There's no escaping it. Even playing it safe, flying under the radar, and holding your breath is failing. Failing to live! So, when you fail—and we all fail constantly—FAIL GLORIOUSLY.

Merriam-Webster's definition of glorious helps raise the stakes on our efforts:

> Glorious:
> 1) possessing or deserving glory
> 2) marked by great beauty or splendor
> 3) delightful, wonderful

In the performing arts, expansive choices are required. "Go big or go home," they say. In our work we ask artists to charge ahead with such conviction that, if they miss their mark, they might leave a cartoon imprint of their body in the wall... as they go through it. (Not literally, unless it's a comedy!)

Failing gloriously reaps many rewards. It allows you to make art out of your failures. (Got lemons? Make lemonade, and add some champagne.) Failing gloriously has the potential to leave others in awe of the risk you have taken. There is also the finer point: the journey, not its desired or intended outcome, is the true lesson. Think of all the amazing art, products, technology, medicines, and more that were discovered as the result of a glorious failure.

Penicillin is a prime example. Alexander Fleming, luckily tapped into his awareness at the time, noticed one of his many contaminated petri dishes was growing a new kind of mold. This wasn't odd except that *this* mold was killing what he was *originally* testing, *Staphylococcus aureus*. The mold turned out to be Penicillin—definitely *not* the original bullseye, and aren't we all healthier for that giant fail?

There are hundreds of these glorious failures in our history, many of them referred to as "accidental discoveries." For fun, go explore with your ensemble the many "failures" we use every day. Here are some to check out: potato chips, Play-dough, Teflon, and brandy. They're just the tip of the iceberg. Wouldn't you like to join the ranks? Let's applaud failure today!

Once you are jazzed on the potential of failing gloriously, try it for yourself in a safe zone first. Cook something new and outrageous completely from scratch. Throw an outfit together that breaks multiple current fashion "rules" and wear it to work. Aim high, and see what exhilarating target you actually hit when you go all-out.

Fail with neon lights blinking around the project. Fail with the brightest colors on and all the microphones pointed at you. Fail with the loudest belly-laugh possible. Record your glaring fiascos.

Using the dictionary's definition again: Fail in a "delightful and wonderful" way. Fail in a way that is marked by great beauty or splendor. Fail in a way that possesses or deserves glory. FAIL GLORIOUSLY!

The world is not broken down only into "successes" or "failures." There are many ways to value and evaluate an experience beyond those two categories. But without leaving open the *possibility* of failure, nothing new can be discovered or accomplished.

In fact, without the *acceptance* or—dare I say it?–*eagerness* to shoot so high that you will most likely fail, nothing new will come.

This acceptance looks the fear of failure straight in the eye and laughs—not at the fear, but at humanity. Every failure, when executed gloriously, has jewels of success inside it. I'm not saying this in a "Well, at least you tried!" kind of way. Yes, that too—but so much more.

The success lies in:

* Commitment to your process.
* Vulnerability of doing all of the above without the certainty of favorable outcome.
* Connection to the project, your passion and the ensemble you're doing it with and for.
* Taking the RISK.
* Divergent thinking, another possibility, tried and tested.
* Awareness of yourself and your surroundings—everything that is influencing this attempt.
* Ownership of *why* and *how* you are "going for it."
* Self-observation that this failure did not kill you. Take note, amygdala.
* Play of trying on something uncertain just for the adventure of it.

* Intentional focus on what you want, regardless of the success or failure.
* Leadership that embodies entering the world full-throttle.
* High-stakes you set, ensuring a glorious attempt, no matter the result.
* Glorious failure! There's no way you could have failed any better! Or could you?

Self-observe and try again. Dig deep on this one.

SELF-OBSERVATION:
Splat! I Meant To Do That
(Thanks, Manifesto)

What do you think about failure?

How do you react when you have failed on your own with no witnesses around?

Does this change when you've failed in front of others?

If so, how?

When, if ever, did a failure turn out to be a success?

How does it feel when you've failed?

How long does the failure stay with you?

How does it stay with you? As physical distress (queasiness or muscle tension)? As mental chatter loops ("I should have...!" "Why did I...?")? As amplified attention to potential failures nearby?

Who do you know or know of, if anyone, that fails gloriously?

How could you, today, embrace failing gloriously in one task?

When was the last time you applauded or supported someone else failing gloriously?

How does it feel to ask yourself these questions?

RHYTHM: HIGH-STAKES
What's the Point?!

It's late evening, or is it early morning? No one can tell anymore. It is only the cards and the held breath that keeps time at this poker table. Players have dropped out left and right, but one woman holds on. "Let's make it interesting, shall we?" she says, sliding all of her remaining chips into the center of the table.

She's all in. The suspended moment of "Now what?" hangs in the air. There is something amazingly powerful, scary and exciting about that act of betting everything you have. It is not a bluff—her intention is clear. This is it.

This is the act of betting on yourself with everything you've got. This could mean:

- Mortgaging the house to go back to school.
- Quitting the 'sure path' to follow your dream.
- Clearly stating your love for someone.
- Asking for what you really want or need in a job interview.
- Stopping everything you're doing to fully listen to your five year-old—with your body, mind, and soul.
- Getting out of bed and right away talking a 20-minute walk outside.

If there is anything in this world
that's worth going "all in" for,
it's You.

You are worth investing in fully. You are more important than the outcome of the game.

If you don't feel that yet, pause now. With your ensemble, brainstorm all the reasons why you are awesome. It's not so much tooting your own horn as conducting a brass band of fabulousness in the key of You. Seriously. Start rattling it off, using your divergent thinking: all the perks, all the potential, all the experience. Do the same exercise for each ensemble member. Laughter and hyperboles will help!

So I might say: "I'm awesome because I can identify voice-over artists in seconds. Whether it's a cartoon movie or a commercial selling cheese I can name that actor. Friends have called it the talent without a home." Fact.

Not to bet on yourself, not to set high-stakes for your actions and goals, is to actively deny your worth. You might think you're merely deciding whether to invest in a project, an idea, a relationship, etc. But these are all extensions of... You.

Let's break down a fictional scenario: Ariel loves architecture and jumps at any opportunity to talk to people about it in casual conversation. Night classes are offered in her area and she loves learning in the company of other people but... The high cost deters her. The time commitment deters her. The fact that she can't see how architecture design classes can advance her banking career deters her... So, she picks up an architecture book at the store. *Ho-Hum.*

The commitment of time, money and acceptance of the unknown are the risks for Ariel. But if Ariel loves architecture, then why not put all her chips in and find a way to make it work? What she did by buying the book (low-stakes) and not the classes (high-stakes) was to tell herself "I'm not worth it. I don't have faith that the higher investment in what I love will bring back dividends. So, I'll get the book, there's no risk there."

Now, for me, this act would usually be followed by a chocolate bar or pizza. Low-Stakes Shame + Instant-Gratification *Yumminess* = Extra 10 Pounds

The return on a high-stakes investment is
increased FAITH: in yourself,
in your ability to make choices
on your terms, and in your ability
to retrain the amygdala.

Through awareness, self-observation, vulnerability and risk-taking, you can decide what's worth going all in for *you*. It's different for everyone. It is absolutely impossible to compare your high-stakes against someone else's.

This is a poker game between you and your fear.

Who's going to win this hand?

SELF-OBSERVATION:
Up the Ante, Manifesto

What would you consider to be a high-stakes bet on You, right now?

How can you up the ante on that bet, even just a little?

Observe any resistance that comes up when you raise the stakes.

Where in your body, mind, and spirit does that resistance—even the slightest holding back or clenching of the teeth—express itself?

Is it in your muscles, your breath, in your mental dialog?

What is something you'd like to do, but haven't yet done?

List small ways that you can "up the ante" for that particular goal.

If resistance kicks in, observe when and why.

What element of the bet is resistance connected to?

How can you, today, raise the stakes on your life and move forward with that choice anyway?

What needs to shift for you to do this?

How does it feel to ask yourself these questions?

CREATIVE
CYCLES

Art Expands Me

and

I Expand My Art

LAUNCH YOUR RITUAL

When you embrace the "What if?", you jump into unknown waters, floating in infinite possibilities. It is wonderfully freeing to get in the water, no matter the temperature or roughness, and to trust yourself to flow with its current, wherever it takes you.

It can also be potentially overwhelming. Infinite possibilities are, well, *infinite*! Consistent access to unlimited success, happiness, creativity, opportunities, and health relies on your faith—faith that your creativity and freedom is, in fact, never-ending. Otherwise, you're really just waiting for the other shoe to drop—making the infinite suddenly finite.

The unlimitedness of your options depends on your faith in unlimitedness.

I use water as a metaphor for infinite creative flow for this main reason: When we are born, we are made of 75% water. Flow is inherent in us. We are in tune to water. This percentage decreases as we age until it settles at closer to 55-60% water, or even less depending on the amount of excess fatty tissue an adult carries. I find this biological fact harmonious with the course of our journey towards creative independence.

We are born in tune with creatively striving for independence. Unfortunately, as we age, the "percentage" of this attunement decreases, and does so even more sharply if we pack on the excess fatty tissue of resistance, assumptions and life-limiting fear. But it doesn't have to slip away.

The infinite creative flow is in us, but it is also something we can immerse ourselves in through play, community and awareness. Just like the individual in the ensemble, we are independent and yet interdependent.

One way to explore, reaffirm or expand your faith in infinite possibilities for your life is to create and perform personal rituals that help you believe "all is possible." Or, if you're a "glass is half-empty" kind of person, rituals, like theatre, can help you "suspend disbelief" long enough to actually jump in the water.

The *Oxford English Dictionary* defines ritual as "a prescribed order of performing religious or other devotional service." This manifesto focuses a devotional service—not to any god, but to the creativity of existence itself and of the independent, intentional life. Here, we use certain rituals as a series of repeatable actions meant to direct the consciousness towards what is greater than fear.

I have a ritual of making a music mix for myself based on the play I am about to create with my ensemble. The music is a mixture of what I find in my research (pieces from the time-period of the show), inspiration (pieces pulled on a more general theme shared with the show, like "Love Unrequited" spanning multiple eras and styles) and emotional motivators (pieces that I know activate the necessary emotion/mood for the work, like a charged punk rock song that revs me up to exuberantly fight my fear of "not being creative enough this time").

The music mix is only one of many personal rituals I have devised. If I break the process of the music mix down, there are really two separate rituals involved. The first is the actual creation of the music mix, where I intentionally and specifically gather and organize my creative energy. The second is the ritual of listening to that mix daily in a variety of settings (getting dressed for rehearsals, in the car, while exercising, before I go to sleep). This ritual shifts me right back into the waters (murky or clear) of my project when I have wandered off seeking safe land.

The other ensemble members also bring their own rituals to the process in the rehearsal room and, through collaborative leadership, we adapt these rituals to support this fresh creative endeavor. Examples of ensemble rituals we regularly use include reading a poem to inspire the work we are about to do, like the ceremonial first pitch at a baseball game or the christening of a ship. Another ritual is physically warming-up with each other by "passing the lead" for a group exercise to each ensemble member, with the expressed rule that it must be taught/led silently. This focuses the ensemble, challenges awareness, trust and vulnerability as well as providing an outlet to explore collaborative leadership and working *As One*. And every rehearsal or workshop has a cyclical ritual: "checking-in" at the beginning and "reinforcing" at the close. (I will talk about both of those soon.)

My ritual of making music mixes came out of a routine of popping on music whenever I had the chance, a running soundtrack for my daily preoccupations. If I could underscore my life, I would: an upbeat tune while I check my mail; sorrowful cellos as I look at my piles of laundry; a good ol' slide whistle as my toddler streaks past me with only his socks on. It was routine, habit, for me to play music as an impromptu underscore. But I usually did not care *what* I was playing before leaving for work—I listened to whatever was in my car. I was aware of the need for music but had not taken ownership in the choices I was making about *what* I was listening to and *how* it could affect my creativity, perspective or mood.

But through my exercises in awareness and self-observation, I realized that I was not using this routine to its fullest potential. There was no higher purpose or journey for the music, it was merely filling a void, like keeping the TV on all day just for the sound it provided.

So, I took the significant components of my routine and consciously sculpted them into a ritual meant to enhance my creative process rather than merely accompaniment for my life as it was. I even started using that ritual to preparing for new experiences seemingly unrelated to my creative work, like a vacation or my son's first year at school. I realized that what works for my creative process could benefit how I create my life. Why keep these rituals and tools under lock and key solely to be used for the creation of art? Why not put them towards the artful living I wanted to achieve?

But the reverse effect can occur too, if you put your creative process on auto-pilot. It won't take long for the motivating quality of your ritual to turn into another deadening routine. Ritual requires open eyes and heart, evoking big-picture perspective. Routine, however, produces blinder-vision; like a ritual, it is made up of repeated set actions, but ones executed *without* heightened awareness, reminiscent of an assembly line.

Routine says, "If I do these prescribed steps, I know exactly what will happen. So much so that I can turn my focus off this and replay in my mind yesterday's argument with my boss." Routine is how you find yourself halfway to work without remembering any part of the transit.

Ritual says, "If I do these prescribed steps, I'm not sure what will happen exactly but I know the bigger goal is for growth." Ritual is what keeps you focused in the gym with the bigger picture of health, honoring the complexity of your body and the joy of taking care of it.

Ritual is beneficial regardless
of the size of your endeavor.
Your unknown waters can be
as intimate as a lazy river
or as wide as the Atlantic Ocean.

The ritual—or vessel—helps you to navigate your liquid journey through the unknown. Floating free in the water works for some, but for many that vast freedom becomes disorienting. Even a small raft can act as a touchstone to why you are on your journey at all. The ritual is that touchstone helping you take leaps of faith into deeper creative waters. Diving off the boat is fun when you know you can climb back on board. The repetition of the ritual allows you to expand and explore. Next time swing off the ship's rigging and get air on that dive!

And don't let Lifeguard Amygdala get too cocky with that whistle. A fin in the water does not *automatically* mean "Shark!" Keep playing, heighten your awareness, use divergent thinking to consider all of the *other* things that "fin" could be before jumping out of the water screaming "Never again! Who told me to jump in there in the first place? I'll kill 'em!" That fin could be an opportunity for play, like a dolphin coming to visit, a responsibility, like garbage needing to be picked up, or a hilarious joke like a kid swimming with a plastic fin on her head. And yes, it could be a shark. But that's life when you are really living it. If you want the safety scenarios of a bath or a pool, it limits your experiences to that which fits into the narrow confines of a bath or pool. There's no chance of swimming with dolphins in there.

Keep all this in mind when constructing your rituals. The rituals you create are always in service of your journey, the ensemble's journey and the needs of the exploration—they are not random. The core structure of the ritual is important—I make a music mix *every time* I work on a show—but how you carry out the ritual will inevitably change depending on your project, your ensemble and your current creative process. Keep observing yourself and tracking your awareness as you perform your ritual to make sure its power to heighten faith is still fulfilling your creative needs.

Working through this book can become a ritual in itself, a way to start your next project fresh inside your creative current. Use the book as a jumping off point to explore the dynamics of each new ensemble you join. Depending on the size of the project or length of time devoted to the ensemble, you can collaboratively decide whether to use the book in its entirety or only specific sections. Both the creation of the ritual and practicing it will serve you. Be mindful during both processes.

Craft your ritual, your vessel, carefully: Taking your journey in an ocean-liner can be luxurious in the Atlantic, but treacherous in a river. And no one wants to have only an inflatable tube in the middle of the ocean, but on a lazy river it is perfect.

Every ritual we know of, no matter how far back it is dated, was created by someone. So why not a new one, now, originating with you?

SELF-OBSERVATION:
Manifesto Incense Are Optional

Do you have rituals already active in your life?

If so, what are they?

Did you come up with the ritual(s), or did you learn from someone else?

Is *play* built into your ritual(s)?

If so, how? If not, why not? Where can it become more playful?

Are there rituals in your life that you observe but do not participate in?

How do you feel about what you observe?

Are there common themes in your ritual(s) that you can find in other ensemble's ritual(s)?

If so, what are they?

What in your life would you like to raise to a heightened level of ritual? For example, how you initiate a project, cook, spring clean or honor an anniversary?

Do you have any creative routines that can be transformed into ritual? For example, how you relax, exercise, self-observe, journal, create your rehearsal process, design research, performance-preparation?

How does it feel to talk about your creative process as linked to ritual or other symbols of faith in the infinite?

How does it feel to ask yourself these questions?

REINFORCING

At the end of every workshop or rehearsal, our company gathers the ensemble for a "reinforcement." This is wonderful ritual handed down by Shakespeare & Co. to Chris when he worked with them.

Much like reinforcing beams in a bridge, this activity supports the journey of each ensemble member. Right before we head out the door, we take a moment to support everyone's participation in the day's process. As we go around the circle, each member has an opportunity to verbally recognize an accomplishment made, either personally or by the ensemble, during rehearsal.

The reinforcements do not have to be monumental, though occasionally they are. For example, if an ensemble member took a noticeable risk, it would mostly likely be reinforced many times by multiple ensemble members.

Examples of reinforcements we often hear are:

"I'd like to reinforce owning my choices."

"I'd like to reinforce that this workshop let me forget about the 'stress' I was under right before I walked in here."

"I'd like to reinforce Matt's improvised song about toothpaste. His humor is incredible and I have no idea how he came up with all those rhymes for plaque."

This is an opportunity to spotlight the individual inside the ensemble. It is also an opportunity for each individual to step up and voice a unique point of view. We have found that this simple ten-minute ritual can solidify an ensemble by validating the time they just spent together.

"Reinforcing" is a way to honor the hard work that occurred in the room, the people who came to the table and the creative discoveries we all made together. What we did together actually happened and we support that now, intentionally and explicitly. It is also a way of leaving that creative, yet fleeting, unit of time in the emptied space to breathe, rest and make itself ready for when we come back the next time.

And even if this particular ensemble does not return the next day, the individuals do. We each return to our creative process, the creative impulse. Reinforcing allows us to start our next project or creative impulse with the insight of the project before. It is Collaborative Leadership at work expanding our individual understanding of the creative process with the multiplicity of awareness operating within and among the ensemble.

Many times ensemble members will return the next day with thoughts on how the reinforcements filtered through the rest of the day. It becomes a strong starting point or "check-in" for the next rehearsal.

Checking-In is a ritual that begins every class or rehearsal we are a part of. It goes hand-in-hand with Reinforcing. All of the members take a minute to succinctly share with the ensemble *how* they are and *where* they are at that very moment. It helps everyone understand the mental, physical and emotional states of the group before we start to create. Stating these things aloud also helps us to own our current states and then let go of whatever is unnecessary to the work we are about to do.

Check-In with your ensemble before you play, and then, before you leave the space, Reinforce. There are many ways to Check-In and Reinforce, so find your own. For example, everyone can Check-In with similes: "I feel like an old shoe whose laces just snapped." Have fun. Get to know each other by expressing and representing yourself more creatively.

This work, like the unfolding of life itself, is a creative process.

I would like to reinforce your efforts, reader, to perceive, question, understand and consciously create your own way of living your life. I also want to reinforce the organic and idiosyncratic way you have approached this manifesto. May it shine your awareness on the ever-evolving and revelatory nature of the creative process.

Give yourself space to breathe with the entire process contained in this Manifesto. Let it sit with you. Feel out your new perspective.

Then come back to the manifesto with a new ensemble or creative project in mind. For example, if all the previous members were your friends, perhaps include work colleagues this time. Or if the previous ensemble was a small group, add more members this time. If your last project was based on individual participation that culminated in an ensemble piece, flip the process. Start with ensemble participation first, then edit it down to individual pieces

Use the manifesto as a way to self-observe your process, to give your ensemble prompts to explore more deeply, and to stay current and honest with how you are working together.

It is important to come back to the key elements of this work because as you expand your creative life, you necessarily sail into uncharted waters and the unknown there can wake up fear again. Think about the vast waters of parenthood: Any parent knows that raising a child requires constant creativity in response to their explorations, which are often conducted quite fearlessly. And so I use the tools I have generated for this manifesto not only for my professional life, but also for my mothering.

As I watch my toddler climb on our foot stool, then run and add his chair on top, and, after that works, go find a box to add to the tower... well, I'm thankful for his amygdala! At some point soon, I hope, fear will remind him of the actual limits of his current motor skills, balance and spatial awareness, and alert him to how close mom is or isn't ("Can she jump and catch me in time?").

But my deeper hope is that Griffin will not stop balancing on furniture simply because of fear: fear of failing, fear of heights, fear of what his parents will say... My hope is that, instead, I will be courageous and vulnerable enough to teach him to engage in the Rhythms of the Revolution to support his exploratory journey. To truly teach him, I'll have to model them. Perhaps he will be Vulnerable and say he needs help, thus engaging his ensemble, Chris and myself (and sometimes Blue Bear his trusty stuffed friend) for Collaborative Leadership. Or he might become Playful and put his stuffed animals up there (they won't be injured if they catapult off) and pretend they are giants. Or he might use Divergent Thinking and decide that the furniture tower is better as a toy holder or Blue Bear's apartment, rather than as an unstable structure to climb.

And more to the point, *I* am able to *enjoy* this whole wobbly adventure because *I* am consciously using these Rhythms. I am consciously living as a creatively independent person. My art, work, relationships and personal outlook have shifted. The fear is there, of course—I have a rightfully vivid imagination which rolls through a dozen 9-1-1 scenarios for my little guy's gravity lab. But I'm retraining my amygdala not to limit his explorations and mine because of fear: fear that he'll come crashing down and injury himself, fear of not being a "good" parent, fear of him doing this when I'm not around, fear of not having the money to replace the footstool if it broke... ugh. Feels heavy even to list them.

It is imperative to self-observe the fear, to name it and declare a fresh independence from it *every time.* You can retrain the amygdala with repetitive exercises in embracing failing gloriously, laughing when you are vulnerable, breathing when you succeed and smiling when you come up against a problem you can't solve— yet.

That's what I keep telling myself as I inch myself closer to Griffin's furniture tower. So far, so good.

There's no end date to this. This work involves the same constant renewal and attention as the other choices we make towards a healthy life—physical, emotional, and mental: vitamins, exercise, healthy foods, laughter, relationships, and so on. Every day that we wake up, we must go through the motions of choosing anew to live according to our values and desires.

Keep it up. Yes, fear may still get the better of you at times, but it will happen less often and each time it will take less time for you to recover from being afraid…

In the hopes that you have at least put one toe in the water, if not performed a full-fledged cannonball, **I would like to reinforce you for:**

* Asking questions to the ensemble to the benefit of us all.
* Making contact.
* Taking a risk.
* Then taking two.
* Spreading the word about that which helps you.
* Owning your choices and passions.
* Observing yourself without judgment.
* Finding the playful routes through this life.
* Being intentional.
* Taking the lead when needed.
* Reassessing the nature of fear.
* Raising the stakes in your life.
* Going all in.
* Rinse and repeat.

SELF-OBSERVATION:
Call In The Reinforcements, Manifesto!

What would you like to reinforce about your ensemble?

What risks have they taken or insight have they shared that's impacted you?

What would you like to reinforce about yourself?

What risks have you taken or insight have you encountered in this process?

Do you reinforce yourself in your daily life? If so, how?

If not, try to reinforce yourself at least once today. Make a conscious effort.

Do you reinforce others in your daily life? If so, how?

If not, try to reinforce an ensemble member at least once today. Make a conscious effort.

How does it feel to ask yourself these questions?

When people ask me what I do for a living…

When someone asks who I am…

Thanks to this manifesto and those that supported its
creation and evolution, I can say,
"I am creatively independent."

HOW DO YOU INTRODUCE YOURSELF?

There's an ensemble of people
waiting to meet you here:
CreativelyIndependent.net/blog

YOUR NOTES_____

INSPIRATION LIST
Always Added To, Never Fully Checked Off:

Find out what or who inspires others on this journey.

This list will keep growing as we explore together. Find the updated list online at Creatively Independent's digital ensemble site: CreativelyIndependent.net/blog.

In the spirit of play, here's a quick scavenger hunt of awesomeness. I won't tell you much about them. The unknown by now, hopefully, is alluring. So, find out about these folks any way you can. Find them now. I'm timing you.

- Brené Brown
- "Cage/Cunningham" Elliot Caplan's documentary on this unique collaboration
- Pema Chodron
- Seth Godin
- Byron Katie
- "Groupthink: The Brainstorming Myth" by Johan Lehrer, The New Yorker
- PBS's "The Music Instinct: Science & Song"
- Sir Ken Robinson
- John Cleese's lecture on Creativity

- TED Talks (I'm a fan of TED roulette sometimes. Just see what Lady Luck has to offer in any field of study.)
- Eckhart Tolle
- Jacques Lecoq
- Complicité's blog "Manuscripts Don't Burn"
- Malcolm Gladwell
- "Breath Made Visible" Ruedi Gerber's documentary on choreographer Anna Halprin
- Twyla Tharp
- Maria Popova's Brain Picker
- PBS's "The Emotional Life"
- Kirby Ferguson's "Everything is a Remix"

If you want to share new inspiring links to books, videos, podcasts and articles, please do at: CreativelyIndependent.net/blog

ABOUT THE AUTHOR
Jess Pillmore

Jess Pillmore is a revolutionary arts educator, co-founder of arts education company Creatively Independent, national director/choreographer, recording singer/songwriter and published writer. She has spent the past fifteen years exploring the common threads within the performing arts that link humanity together. Those fundamental threads make it possible for her company to teach and create with artists of all ages and skill levels since 2001.

Jess's artistic explorations include three nationally released folk rock albums, a short collaborative film with HitRECord screened at Sundance Festival 2012, an upcycled knitwear line, A Second Chance , featured in two national magazines and an upcoming book on ensemble driven Shakespeare for arts education.

As a student, Jess has had the honor of training with cutting edge artists in their fields: Seth Godin, Kathleen Marshall, Susan Schulman, Gregory Hines, k. Jenny Jones, Kira Obolensky and Devora Neumark.

MFA Interdisciplinary Arts (Goddard College)
BA Theatre (FSU)

ABOUT CREATIVELY INDEPENDENT
Revolutionary Arts Education

CI is an ensemble based arts and education company touring 250+ days/year reaching over 3,000 students/ year of all levels. Combined, the Co–Artistic Directors, Chris Beaulieu and Jess Pillmore, have directed/ choreographed 60+ shows (Off–Broadway, Fringe, International, Regional & Educational). We have presented at multiple national/international festivals and companies: Kennedy Center American College Theatre Festival (SE Region), Performing the World (NYC), Int'l Schools Theatre Assoc., Williamstown Theatre Festival's Greylock Project, Circus Smirkus and Dell' Arte International Co. CI's Artistic Directors have trained and worked with Dell' Arte, Shakespeare & Co., Tony Award winning artists (Ann Reinking, Susan Schulman and Kathleen Marshall), and the Society of American Fight Directors.

Jess received Best Female Combatant and Best Unarmed at the National Workshop and Chris received the high honor of the Paddy Crean Award. Our at–risk community work, Living Inside/Art in Jail, was recognized by the National Endowment for the Arts.

CI focuses on new works including folk rock musical, "It's All Right Now", Commedia piece, "The Greatest Story Never Told" and "Self-Observation" a performative lecture on presence and awareness.

In 2011, CI created an artist retreat in the Blue Ridge Mountains of Virginia. This retreat offers summer intensives in creativity, teacher-training on expanding progressive education utilizing the arts. There are facilities for ensembles to rent in which to create in the beauty and quiet of SW Virginia.

CREATIVELY INDEPENDENT SERVICES

The manifesto emerged from our performing arts workshops geared towards any age, skill level and interest. Creatively Independent tours internationally as guest directors, choreographers, creative consultants and teaching artists in the following intensives:

Being Present - You are enough. Find your neutral stance, heightened awareness and honest presence. Own what makes you unique in order to boldly create.

As One - Learn how to feel the group's intention and commit to your own individual intention. Utilize the group, improvisation and heightened sense of awareness.

The Tangible Objective - Explore the feeling of "have-to" in your muscles, heart, breath and spine, no matter what the objective is, in order to understand honest need, longing, failure and success.

Performance Intention - Amplify your commitment and focus. Hone in on your process and your intention. Feel what it means to step into higher stakes.

Ensemble Devising Techniques - Whether in art, business or daily life, there are many ways to create as a group. Bust through assumptions of how to create, what to create and with whom.

Overlaying - Develop x-ray vision to find the bones of a scene or relationship. Discover the bare essentials and find potential overlays of metaphors or textures in order create a multi-layered and unique interpretation.

More information about booking our services can be found at CreativelyIndependent.net

22723489R00094

Made in the USA
Charleston, SC
01 October 2013